200 FISH & SHELLFISH RECIPES

200 FISH & SHELLFISH RECIPES

THE DEFINITIVE COOK'S COLLECTION WITH OVER 200 FABULOUS RECIPES

LINDA DOESER

HERMES
HOUSE

This edition is published by Hermes House,
an imprint of Anness Publishing Ltd, Blaby Road, Wigston,
Leicestershire LE18 4SE; info@anness.com

www.hermeshouse.com; www.annesspublishing.com

If you like the images in this book and would like to investigate using
them for publishing, promotions or advertising, please visit our website
www.practicalpictures.com for more information.

© Anness Publishing Ltd 2012

A CIP record for this book is available from the British Library.

Publisher: Joanna Lorenz
Cookery Editor: Linda Doeser
Copy Editor: Leslie Viney
Designer: Mason Linklater
Illustrator: Madeleine David

NOTES
For all recipes, quantities are given in both metric and imperial measures
and, where appropriate, in standard cups and spoons. Follow one set of
measures, but not a mixture, because they are not interchangeable.
Standard spoon and cup measures are level.
1 tsp = 5ml, 1 tbsp = 15ml, 1 cup = 250ml/8fl oz.
Australian standard tablespoons are 20ml. Australian readers should
use 3 tsp in place of 1 tbsp for measuring small quantities.
American pints are 16fl oz/2 cups. American readers should use
20fl oz/2.5 cups in place of 1 pint when measuring liquids.
Electric oven temperatures in this book are for conventional ovens.
When using a fan oven, the temperature will probably need to be
reduced by about 10–20°C/20–40°F. Since ovens vary, you should
check with your manufacturer's instruction book for guidance.
Medium (US large) eggs are used unless otherwise stated.

Main front cover image shows Trout Wrapped in a Blanket
– for recipe, see page 201.

PUBLISHER'S NOTE
Although the advice and information in this book are believed to be
accurate and true at the time of going to press, neither the authors nor
the publisher can accept any legal responsibility or liability for any
errors or omissions that may have been made nor for any inaccuracies
nor for any loss, harm or injury that comes about from following
instructions or advice in this book.

CONTENTS

❧

Introduction

Rightly called the 'harvest of the sea', fish, shellfish and other seafood offer almost endless possibilities for delicious, nutritious and healthy meals. There are a vast number of different ways of preparing fish: grilled, baked, steamed, served in a creamy sauce, combined with fruit or vegetables, curried, wrapped in parcels or cold with salads, to name just a few. The recipes in this book have been inspired by dishes from all over the world and explore interesting ways with both familiar and unfamiliar varieties.

The book begins with an introduction to the main types of fish, with some helpful hints on buying and storing fish and useful equipment. This is followed by a step-by-guide to techniques, including trimming, gutting, skinning, scaling, preparing steaks and cutlets and filleting. Techniques for seafood follow, with preparing mussels and clams, opening oysters and scallops and deveining prawns. This section is completed with a guide to basic cooking techniques: poaching, steaming, grilling, and coating and frying. The recipes themselves are divided into seven chapters: Soups, Starters, Salads, Pasta and Rice, Fried and Grilled Dishes, Pies and Bakes, and Casseroles and Stews.

Besides being easy and quick to prepare, seafood is highly nutritious and plays an important role in the modern cook's approach to preparing healthy meals. Modern research confirms the value of fish in the diet for lowering cholesterol levels, as well as offering many other health benefits.

More than anything else, fish – whether freshwater or from the sea – offers immense scope to the creative cook. The recipes here range from the simple, yet delicious, to the elaborate and self-indulgent. There are recipes to suit all tastes and budgets and dishes suitable for every occasion.

Types of Fish and Seafood

Fish can be almost any size and colour and range from the solitary bottom-dwellers in the deep ocean to the huge shoals of coastal fish. However, from the cook's point of view, they fall into three categories: round fish, flat fish (both sea types) and freshwater fish.

Round fish

This large group, which includes such familiar varieties as herring, cod, haddock, whiting, pollack, anchovy, sprat, sardine, grouper and mullet, are distinguished by having a rounded body, eyes on either side of the head and by swimming with the dorsal (back) fin uppermost. As well as bony fish, it includes cartilaginous species, such as dogfish and shark. Round fish are usually sold whole, in fillets or in steaks. Many of the oily varieties, such as mackerel and tuna, are delicious grilled or fried. White fish, such as whiting, which has a particularly delicate flavour and fine texture, may be fried or poached. Firm-fleshed fish is ideal for baking or stuffing. Salmon are included in this group, although part of their life cycle is spent in fresh water.

Flat fish

This group, which includes, sole (lemon and Dover), plaice, dab, witch, flounder, brill, turbot and halibut, swim on one side and have both eyes on the same side of the head. Usually the lower, blind side is paler than the upper side of the fish. Most flat fish, with the exception of halibut, turbot and skate, is sold whole or in fillets. The very large varieties are usually available as steaks and only the wings of skate are sold. The shallow bodies of flat fish and their generally firm but tender and flavourful flesh make them ideal for grilling or sautéing.

Freshwater fish

Apart from trout, which nowadays is readily available as a farm fish, these are not so frequently seen as seawater fish. Favourite freshwater fish include bream, perch, St Peter's fish, char, pike, carp, freshwater catfish and eel.

Crustaceans

This group covers all the aquatic creatures, both fresh- and seawater, with five pairs of legs: lobster, crab, prawn, crayfish and crawfish. They tend to have firm, sweet flesh and many have heavy front claws or pincers. The head and body are usually, but not invariably, enclosed in a tough shell or carapace. Prawns are often sold cooked, although they are also available raw. Crabs and lobsters are fresher and more delicious if they are bought live, but some people find it distressing to kill them. Prawns are especially delicious gently sautéed, while lobster is particularly suited to delicate poaching.

Shellfish

This group includes single-shelled molluscs, such as the whelk and winkle, and the more popular bivalves, such as oysters, mussels, clams and scallops. It also includes the family to which squid, cuttle-fish and octopus belong. Some shellfish, especially oysters, are usually eaten raw in their own juices from the shell. Cockles and razor shells may also be eaten raw, but are good in soups too. Mussels and clams are delicious steamed in their own juices or in white wine

and lemon juice, and scallops are often poached. All shellfish should be bought on the day they are going to be eaten as they go off extremely quickly.

Buying and storing

When choosing fish, it is the appearance and smell that reflect its condition. When buying whole fish, look for shining skin, bright colour, pink gills and full bright

eyes with black pupils and trans-parent corneas. The flesh should be soft, but springy and the body should be firm. Genuinely fresh fish has clean, pleasant odour, so reject any with the suggestion of a 'fishy smell'. The only exceptions are shark and skate. This is because their flesh contains a chemical that breaks down after death to yield ammonia, which has an irritating smell. It is best to store skate and shark for a couple of days after they have been caught before preparing and cooking.

Shellfish deteriorate more rapidly than fish. Many, such as clams and mussels, are sold alive for this reason. Cooked crab, lobster and prawns are available and some types of shellfish are sold frozen. However, neither has quite the same flavour and texture as fresh seafood. As a general rule, you can tell if seafood is fresh because it does not smell.

Seafood will keep fresh for no longer than one day if stored in the refrigerator. Wrap it loosely in greaseproof paper or foil to prevent its smell from penetrating other foods. Fish freezes well, but you should be sure that it really is fresh and has not already been frozen on the fishing ship and thawed before sale.

Equipment

Clockwise from top left: fish grid for the barbecue, fish kettle, whole fish grid for the barbecue, fish terrine mould, divided fish lifter, scaler, large fish slice, fish slice, fish platter, filleting knife, strong scissors, oyster knife, zester, skewers, fish-shaped mousse mould.

Fish-shaped mousse mould
An attractive way to present a cold mousse or fish mould.

Large fish slice
Useful for lifting whole fish and large fillets lengthways.

Oyster knife
A purpose-made tool for opening tightly closed oyster shells. You can prize the shells apart with the strong blade.

Scaler
This is perfect for scraping off stubborn scales. Alternatively, you can use a blunt knife. In either case, this is best done under running water.

Skewers
Use for brochettes to cook on the barbecue or under the grill.

Strong scissors
Good for trimming fins and tails.

Whole fish grid for the barbecue
This is designed for cooking a whole large fish on the barbecue. Gut before cooking and season well. Wrap in large sprigs of fresh herbs, such as rosemary. Turn over halfway through the cooking time.

Zester
A quick method to add citrus fruit zest to any stuffing or marinade or to make a quick, fresh garnish.

Divided fish lifter
A useful gadget which opens out so that you can lift a whole fish or large fillet of fish with one hand without breaking it.

Filleting knife
A long, flexible knife is essential for skinning and filleting fish, as it can curve around the shape of the body, its bones and flesh. Keep the knife as sharp as possible.

Fish grid for the barbecue
This circular grid is ideal for cooking whole small fish, such as sardines, on the barbecue. Place the fish in the shaped grid and position on the barbecue, turning the whole grid over halfway through the cooking time.

Fish kettle
This elongated saucepan, fitted with a trivet or rack, is used to poach large, whole fish, such as salmon. Place the fish on the trivet with water in the base of the kettle and make sure that the lid is tight fitting. Poach over two hob rings or in the oven. Kettles are available in different sizes and there is even a specially shaped kettle made for poaching turbot, but this is really not essential equipment for a domestic kitchen.

Fish platter
A large flat platter essential for displaying whole fish. It makes an attractive centrepiece, particularly on a buffet table.

Fish slice
Good for lifting fish fillets or single portions of fish.

Fish terrine mould
Ideal for large fish pâtés or terrines. Always cook in a *bain marie*, that is, placed in a large roasting tin, filled halfway up the side of the terrine mould with boiling water. Cast iron moulds are ideal for cooking the terrine, but make sure that they are always covered with the lid and line the mould with greaseproof paper to allow for ease of turning out. Serve the terrine sliced.

Trimming Round Fish

1 With a pair of heavy scissors, cut away the fins on either side of the fish, then cut away the ventral or belly fins.

2 Cut away the dorsal fins along the back.

3 Trim the tail by cutting a 'V' shape into it.

Gutting Round Fish Through the Stomach

1 With a medium knife, slit the underside of the fish from the gills to the small ventral opening. Take care not to insert the knife too far.

2 Carefully loosen the stomach contents from the cavity with your fingers and pull them out.

3 Using a teaspoon, scrape along the vertebrae in the cavity to remove the kidney.

4 Pull out the gills. Wash the cavity with cold water.

Gutting Round Fish

1 With a heavy pair of scissors, cut along the fish's belly.

2 Remove the insides with your fingers and wash the cavity.

Boning Round Fish for Stuffing

1 Gut the fish through the stomach as described on the previous page.

2 Slit the fish on either side of the backbone, cutting the flesh away from the bone until it is completely detached.

3 With a heavy pair of scissors, snip the backbone once at the head and once at the tail.

4 Lift out the bone.

Boning a Round Fish Through the Stomach

1 Gut the fish through the stomach as previously described. Continue the stomach slit on one side of the backbone as far as the tail.

2 Open the cavity and remove the insides.

3 Clean the insides of the fish, wiping away any remaining blood or guts.

4 Open the cavity and, with the blade of the knife, cut away the loose inside bones that line the flesh.

5 Turn the fish over and slit the flesh at the base of the backbone on the other side.

6 With the blade of the knife, cut loose the inside bones lining the flesh in the same way as the first side.

7 Carefully loosen the backbone of the fish completely.

8 With scissors, snip the backbone at the head and the tail.

9 Carefully peel the backbone away from the flesh with any inside bones.

10 The head can be kept and the two side fillets rolled in spirals, skin side inwards. Alternatively, fold the skin outwards and tuck the tail inside.

11 Alternatively, the head and skin can be removed and the fillets rolled or cooked flat.

Cutting Steaks and Cutlets

1 With a large, sharp knife, slice the fish across, at a right angle to the backbone, into slices of the desired thickness.

2 If necessary, cut through the backbone with kitchen scissors or a knife with a serrated blade.

Filleting Round Fish

1 Holding the knife horizontally, slit the skin from head to tail along one side of the backbone.

3 Holding the knife flat and keeping the blade in contact with the bone, cut away the flesh from head to tail in a continuous slicing motion.

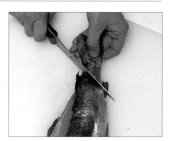

5 Trim off the tail.

2 Cut down to the backbone just behind the fish's head.

4 Cut the backbone at the tail end with scissors.

6 Cut the fish into two fillets.

Skinning a Fillet

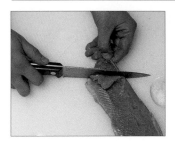

1 Secure the fillet with salt on a chopping board. Insert a sharp, flexible knife at the end of the fillet and hold securely.

2 Working in a cutting motion against the skin, move the knife along the fillet.

3 Continue until the skin has been completely removed from the flesh.

Boning Flat Fish

1 Using a flexible knife, cut along the backbone.

2 Cut the flesh away from the bones, holding the knife almost parallel to them.

3 Cut to the edge of the transverse bones, but do not remove the fillet completely.

4 Turn the fish over and repeat for the opposite fillet.

5 Fold both fillets out.

6 Using a strong pair of scissors, cut the bones along the edges.

7 Loosen the bones away from the flesh.

8 With kitchen scissors, snip the backbone at both the head and the tail ends.

9 Lift the backbone at the tail end and pull, stripping it from the flesh underneath.

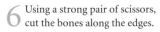

Filleting Flat Fish

3 Turn the fish over and cut a straight line from the tail to the head as before.

4 Work the flesh away from the bones as described in steps 1 and 2, and then repeat with the fourth fillet.

1 With a sharp knife, cut around the edge of the fish to outline the shape of the fillets. Cut a straight line from the tail to the head along the spine through the bone. Keeping the knife almost flat, slip it between the flesh and the rib bones.

2 Cut away the fillet, using a stroking motion and keeping the knife flat. Continue cutting until the fillet and flesh against the fins has been detached with the skin in one piece. Continue with the other fillet.

Skinning Flat Fish

1 Lay the fish on a chopping board, dark side uppermost. With a sharp knife held at an angle, cut across the skin where the tail joins the body, taking care not to cut all the way through.

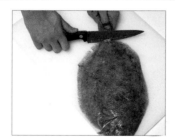

2 With the knife still held at an angle, start to cut. Keep the fish secure on the board with some salt and gradually prise the flap of skin away from the flesh. When you have a good flap of skin, grasp it with one hand and hold the other end of the fish with your other hand. Firmly pull the skin towards the head.

Fish Stock

675g/1½lb head, bones and trimmings
   from white fish
1 onion, sliced
2 celery sticks with leaves, chopped
1 carrot, sliced
½ lemon, sliced (optional)
1 bay leaf
3–4 fresh parsley sprigs
6 black peppercorns
1.3 litres/2¼ pints/5½ cups water
120ml/4fl oz/½ cup dry white wine

1 Rinse the fish heads, bones and trimmings under cold running water. Put them in a large saucepan with the vegetables, lemon, if using, herbs, peppercorns, water and wine. Bring to the boil, skimming the surface frequently. Reduce the heat and simmer for 25 minutes.

2 Strain the stock, but do not press down on the contents of the strainer. If you are not using the stock immediately, leave to cool and then refrigerate. Fish stock should be used within 2 days. It may be frozen and kept for up to 3 months.

Preparing Mussels and Clams

Molluscs, such as mussels and clams, should be eaten very fresh and should be alive when you buy and cook them (unless they have been shelled and frozen or are canned). You can tell if they are alive because their shells are tightly closed. Any that are open, should shut at once when tapped sharply with a knife. Any that do not close or that have broken shells should be discarded.

If you have collected the shellfish yourself, leave them to stand in a bucket of sea water for several hours, changing the water once or twice. Do not use fresh water, as it will kill them. Add one or two handfuls of cornmeal or flour to the water to help clean the stomachs of the shellfish. Shellfish bought from a shop will already have been purged of sand.

1 Scrub the shells with a stiff brush and rinse well. This can be done under cold running water.

2 Pull off the 'beards' (their anchor threads) with the help of a small knife. Rinse well.

3 To steam, put a little dry white wine or water in a large saucepan, together with any flavourings specified in the recipe. Add the mussels or clams, cover tightly and bring to the boil. Cook for 5–10 minutes, or until the shells open, shaking the pan from time to time. Discard any that do not open.

4 Serve the shellfish in the shells or shell them before using. Strain the cooking liquid, which includes the liquor from the shells, and spoon it over the shellfish or use it as the basis for a sauce.

5 To open a live clam or mussel, hold it in one hand with the hinge in your palm. Insert the side of a clam or oyster knife blade between the shell halves and work it round to cut through the hinge muscle.

6 Open the shell and cut the clam or mussel free of the shell. Do this over a bowl to catch all the liquor from the shell.

Opening and Cleaning Scallops

1 To open the shell, hold the scallop with the flat shell uppermost. Probe between the shells with a short knife to find a small opening. Insert the blade and run it across the roof of the shell.

2 Separate the two halves of the shell, and pull apart.

3 Slide the blade under the greyish outer rim of the flesh, called the skirt, to free the scallop. Pull away the muscle with a small knife. Use the trimmed scallop, whole or halved, for cooking.

Opening Oysters

1 Place the oyster, wrapped in a clean napkin or tea towel, on a firm surface with the flatter shell uppermost and the hinge towards you. Holding the oyster with one hand, insert the tip of an oyster knife into the gap in the hinge.

2 Twist the blade to snap the shells apart.

3 Continue to hold the oyster firmly in the cloth and slide the blade along the inside of the upper shell to sever the muscle that holds the shell together. Discard the top shell and lift the lower rounded shell off the napkin, making sure the liquid in it does not spill. Clean any bits of broken shell with the point of the knife.

4 Grip the lower shell firmly with your fingers. Cutting towards yourself, run the blade under the oyster to sever the muscle attaching it to the lower shell and free it.

Preparing and Deveining Prawns

Prawns may be cooked in their shells, but are often peeled first. The shells can be used to make an aromatic stock. The intestinal vein that runs down the back is usually removed from large prawns, mainly because of its appearance, but also because it may contain grit which makes it unpleasant to eat. Prawns may be sold with the heads on. These are easily pulled off with the fingers and will enhance the flavour of stock made with their shells.

1 Holding the prawn firmly in one hand, pull off the legs with the fingers of the other hand.

2 Peel the shell away from the body. When you reach the tail, hold the body and pull away the tail; the shell will come off with it. Alternatively, you can leave the tail on the prawn and just remove the body shell.

3 Make a shallow cut down the centre of the curved back of the prawn. Pull out the black vein with a cocktail stick or your fingers.

4 To make butterfly prawns, cut along the deveining slit to split open the prawn, without cutting all the way through. Open up the prawn flat.

5 To devein prawns in their shells, insert a cocktail stick crossways in several places along the back where the shell overlaps to lift out the vein.

Poaching

Whole fish, large and small, as well as fillets, cutlets and steaks, are excellent poached because the gentle cooking gives succulent results. Poached fish can be served hot or cold with a wide variety of sauces. The poaching liquid may be used as a basis for the sauce.

1 To oven poach small, whole fish, fillets, cutlets or steaks, place the fish in a buttered, flame-proof dish that is large enough to hold the pieces in a single layer. Pour in enough liquid to come two-thirds of the way up the sides of the fish.

2 Add any flavourings specified in the recipe. Press a piece of buttered, greaseproof paper on top to keep in the moisture.

3 Set the dish over moderate heat and bring the liquid just to the boil. Transfer the dish to a preheated oven at 180°C/350°F/ Gas 4 and poach until the fish is just cooked. To test, with the tip of a sharp knife, make a small cut into the thickest part of the fish, ideally near a bone. The flesh should be slightly translucent.

4 To poach whole fish, fillets, cutlets or steaks on the hob, put large whole fish on the rack in a fish kettle or set on a piece of muslin that can be used like a hammock. Small whole fish, fillets, cutlets and steaks may be poached in a fish kettle on a rack or set directly in a wide saucepan or frying pan.

5 Prepare the poaching liquid – water, milk, wine or stock – in the fish kettle, a large casserole, a roasting tin, a wide saucepan or frying pan, as appropriate. Set the rack in the kettle or the muslin hammock in the casserole or tin. Add more liquid if necessary.

6 Cover the kettle or casserole and bring the liquid just to the boil. Reduce the heat and simmer very gently until the fish is cooked.

Steaming

This simple, moist-heat method of cooking is ideal for fish and shellfish. If you do not have a steamer, it is easy to improvise.

1 Using a steamer, arrange the fish on the rack in the steamer and set over boiling water. Cover and steam until done.

2 For Chinese-style steaming, arrange the fish on a heatproof plate that will fit inside a bamboo steamer or wok. Put the plate in the steamer or on the rack in the wok, set over boiling water, cover and steam until done.

3 For steaming larger fish and fillets, arrange the fish on a rack in a roasting tin of boiling water or on a plate set on the rack. Cover tightly with foil and steam until done.

4 To steam in foil, wrap the fish and seasonings in foil, sealing well, and set on a rack in the steamer or in a large roasting tin of boiling water. Steam until done.

Grilling

1 To grill small, whole oily fish, boned and butterflied fish, fillets, cutlets and steaks that are at least 1cm/½in thick or cubes of fish on skewers, rinse the fish and pat it dry with kitchen paper. Marinate the fish if the recipe suggests this.

2 Preheat the grill with the grill pan in place. When hot, lightly brush the hot pan with oil. Arrange the fish in the pan in a single layer, skin side down, brush the fish with butter, oil or a basting mixture, according to the recipe.

3 Set the fish under the grill, 7.5–10cm/3–4in from the heat. Thin pieces should be closer to the heat for a shorter time than thicker ones. Grill, basting once or twice and turning if the recipe specifies, until the fish is done.

4 To grill leaner, small whole fish, steaks, cutlets and fillets that are at least 1cm/½in thick and prepared for cooking as above, arrange in a buttered, flameproof dish. Add a little liquid – wine, stock or court bouillon – just to cover the base of the dish. Brush the fish with butter, oil or a basting mixture, according to the recipe. Grill as above, without turning the fish.

Coating and Frying

1 Lightly beat an egg in a shallow dish. Spread some flour on a plate or sheet of grease-proof paper and season with salt and freshly ground black pepper or ingredients as specified in the recipe. Spread fine breadcrumbs or crushed water biscuits on another plate or sheet of greaseproof paper.

2 To egg and crumb large pieces of fish, dip the fish first in the seasoned flour, turning to coat both sides lightly and evenly. Shake or brush off excess flour.

3 Next, dip the floured fish in the egg, turning to moisten both sides.

4 Dip the fish in the crumbs, turning to coat evenly. Press to help the crumbs adhere. Shake or pat off excess crumbs. Chill in the refrigerator for at least 20 minutes to set the coating.

5 To egg and crumb small pieces of fish, strips of fish fillet, goujons or prawns, put the crumbs in a plastic bag. After dipping the fish in seasoned flour and egg, toss a few pieces at a time in the plastic bag of crumbs.

6 To pan fry, heat some oil or a mixture of oil and butter in a frying pan, using enough to coat the base of the pan in a thin layer or according to recipe instructions. When it is very hot, put the fish in the pan in a single layer. Fry until golden brown on both sides and the fish is done. Drain on kitchen paper before serving.

7 To deep-fry, half fill a deep pan with oil and heat it to 190°C/375°F. Gently lower the coated pieces of fish into the hot oil, frying them only a few at a time. Fry until golden brown, turning them occasionally, so that they cook evenly. Remove and drain thoroughly on kitchen paper before serving.

SOUPS

Smoked Haddock and Potato Soup

The traditional name for this soup is 'cullen skink'. A cullen is the 'seatown' or port district of a town, while 'skink' means stock or broth.

Serves 6

1 finnan haddock, about 350g/12oz

1 onion, chopped

bouquet garni

900ml/1½ pints/3¾ cups water

500g/1¼ lb potatoes, quartered

600ml/1 pint/2½ cups milk

40g/1½oz butter

salt and freshly ground black pepper

snipped chives, to garnish

1 Put the haddock, onion, bouquet garni and water into a large saucepan and bring to the boil. Skim the scum from the surface, then cover the pan. Reduce the heat and poach for 10–15 minutes, until the haddock flakes easily.

COOK'S TIP
Finnan haddock is a small, whole fish that has been soaked in brine and then cold smoked.

2 Lift the haddock from the pan, using a fish slice, and remove the skin and bones. Flake the flesh and reserve. Return the skin and bones to the pan and simmer, uncovered, for 30 minutes.

3 Strain the fish stock and return to the pan, then add the potatoes and simmer for about 25 minutes, or until tender. Remove the potatoes from the pan using a slotted spoon. Add the milk to the pan and bring to the boil.

4 Meanwhile, mash the potatoes with the butter, then whisk into the milk in the pan until thick and creamy. Add the flaked fish to the pan and adjust the seasoning. Sprinkle with chives and serve at once with crusty bread.

Corn and Scallop Chowder

Fresh ears of corn are ideal for this chowder, although canned or frozen corn also works well. This soup makes a perfect lunch dish.

INGREDIENTS

Serves 4–6

2 ears of corn or 200g/7oz frozen or
    canned corn
600ml/1pint/2½ cups milk
15g/½oz butter or margarine
1 small leek or onion, chopped
1 small garlic clove, crushed
40g/1½oz smoked lean bacon,
    finely chopped
1 small green pepper, seeded and diced
1 celery stick, chopped
1 medium potato, diced
15ml/1 tbsp plain flour
300ml/½ pint/1¼ cups chicken or
    vegetable stock
4 scallops
115g/4oz cooked fresh mussels
pinch of paprika
150ml/¼ pint/⅔ cup single
    cream (optional)
salt and freshly ground black pepper

1 Using a sharp knife, slice down the ears of the corn to remove the kernels. Place half of the kernels in a food processor or blender and process with a little of the milk.

2 Melt the butter or margarine in a large saucepan and gently fry the leek or onion, garlic and bacon for 4–5 minutes until the leek is soft but not browned. Add the green pepper, chopped celery and diced potato and sweat over low heat for a further 3–4 minutes, stirring frequently.

3 Stir in the flour and cook for 1–2 minutes until the mixture is golden and frothy. Gradually stir in the milk and corn mixture, stock, the remaining milk and corn kernels and seasoning.

4 Bring to the boil, then reduce the heat and simmer, partially covered, for 15–20 minutes until the vegetables are tender.

5 Pull the corals away from the scallops and slice the white flesh into 5mm/¼ in slices. Stir the scallops into the soup, cook for 4 minutes and then stir in the corals, mussels and paprika. Heat through for a few minutes and then stir in the cream, if using. Adjust the seasoning to taste and serve.

Classic Italian Fish Soup

Liguria is famous for its fish soups. In this one the fish are cooked in a broth with vegetables and then puréed. This soup can also be used to dress pasta.

INGREDIENTS

Serves 6

1kg/2¼lb mixed fish or fish pieces, such as
    coley, dogfish, whiting, red mullet,
    pollock or cod
90ml/6 tbsp olive oil, plus extra to serve
1 medium onion, finely chopped
1 stick celery, chopped
1 carrot, chopped
60ml/4 tbsp chopped fresh parsley
175ml/6fl oz/¾ cup dry white wine
3 medium tomatoes, skinned and chopped
2 garlic cloves, finely chopped
1.5 litres/2½ pints/6¼ cups boiling water
salt and freshly ground black pepper
rounds of French bread, to serve

1 Scale and clean the fish, discarding all the innards, but leaving the heads on. Cut into large pieces. Rinse well in cool water.

2 Heat the oil in a large saucepan and add the onion. Cook over low to moderate heat until it begins to soften. Stir in the celery and carrot, and cook for 5 minutes more. Add the parsley.

3 Pour in the wine, raise the heat, and cook until it reduces by about half. Stir in the tomatoes and garlic. Cook for 3–4 minutes, stirring occasionally. Pour in the boiling water, and bring back to the boil. Cook over moderate heat for 15 minutes.

4 Stir in the fish, and simmer for 10–15 minutes, or until the fish are tender. Season with salt and pepper.

5 Remove the fish from the soup with a slotted spoon. Discard the heads and any bones. Purée in a food processor. Taste for seasoning. If the soup is too thick, add a little more water.

6 To serve, heat the soup to simmering. Toast the rounds of French bread, and sprinkle with olive oil. Place 2 or 3 in the base of each soup plate before pouring over the soup.

Shellfish with Seasoned Broth

Leave one or two mussels and prawns in their shells to add an extra touch to this elegant dish.

Serves 4

675g/1½lb mussels, scrubbed and
   debearded
1 small fennel bulb, thinly sliced
1 onion, thinly sliced
1 leek, thinly sliced
1 small carrot, cut in julienne strips
1 garlic clove
1 litre/1⅔ pints/4 cups water
pinch of curry powder
pinch of saffron
1 bay leaf
450g/1lb large raw prawns, peeled
450g/1lb small shelled scallops
175g/6oz cooked lobster meat,
   sliced (optional)
salt and freshly ground black pepper
15–30ml/1–2 tbsp chopped fresh chervil
   or parsley, to serve

2 Put the fennel, onion, leek, carrot and garlic in a saucepan and add the water, reserved mussel liquid, spices and bay leaf. Bring to the boil, skimming any foam that rises to the surface, then reduce the heat and simmer gently, covered, for 20 minutes until the vegetables are tender. Remove the garlic clove.

3 Add the prawns, scallops and lobster meat, if using, then after 1 minute, add the mussels. Simmer gently for about 3 minutes until the scallops are opaque and all the shellfish are heated through. Adjust the seasoning, then ladle into a heated tureen and sprinkle with the chervil or parsley.

1 Put the mussels in a large heavy saucepan or flameproof casserole, cover with water and cook, tightly covered, over a high heat for 4–6 minutes until the shells open, shaking the pan or casserole occasionally. When cool enough to handle, discard any mussels that did not open and remove the rest from their shells. Strain the cooking liquid through a muslin-lined sieve and reserve.

Bouillabaisse

Perhaps the most famous of all Mediterranean fish soups, this recipe, originating from Marseilles in the south of France, is a rich and colourful mixture of fish and shellfish, flavoured with tomatoes, saffron and orange.

INGREDIENTS

Serves 4–6

1.5kg/3-3½lb mixed fish and raw shellfish, such as red mullet, John Dory, monkfish, red snapper, whiting, large raw prawns and clams
225g/8oz well-flavoured tomatoes
pinch of saffron strands
90ml/6 tbsp olive oil
1 onion, sliced
1 leek, sliced
1 celery stick, sliced
2 garlic cloves, crushed
1 bouquet garni
1 strip orange rind
2.5ml/½ tsp fennel seeds
15ml/1 tbsp tomato purée
10ml/2 tsp Pernod
salt and freshly ground black pepper
4–6 thick slices French bread and 45ml/ 3 tbsp chopped fresh parsley, to serve

1 Remove the heads, tails and fins from the fish and set the fish aside. Put the trimmings in a large pan, with 1.2 litres/2 pints/ 5 cups water. Bring to the boil, and simmer for 15 minutes. Strain, and reserve the liquid.

2 Cut the fish into large chunks. Leave the shellfish in their shells. Scald the tomatoes, then drain and refresh in cold water. Peel and roughly chop them. Soak the saffron in 15–30ml/1–2 tbsp hot water.

3 Heat the oil in a large pan, add the onion, leek and celery and cook until softened. Add the garlic, bouquet garni, orange rind, fennel seeds and tomatoes, then stir in the saffron and soaking liquid and the fish stock. Season with salt and pepper, then bring to the boil and simmer for 30–40 minutes.

4 Add the shellfish and boil for about 6 minutes. Add the fish and cook for a further 6–8 minutes, until it flakes easily.

5 Using a slotted spoon, transfer the fish to a warmed serving platter. Keep the liquid boiling, to allow the oil to emulsify with the broth. Add the tomato purée and Pernod, then check the seasoning. To serve, place a slice of French bread in the base of each soup bowl, pour the broth over the top and serve the fish separately, sprinkled with the parsley.

COOK'S TIP

Saffron comes from the orange and red stigmas of a type of crocus. These must be harvested by hand and it requires about 250,000 crocus flowers for a yield of 500g/1¼lb saffron. Consequently, it is extremely expensive – the highest-priced spice in the world. However, its slightly bitter flavour and pleasantly sweet aroma are unique and cannot be replaced by any other spice. It is an essential ingredient in all tradi- tional versions of bouillabaisse and should not be omitted.

Prawn Bisque

The classic French method for making a bisque requires pushing the shellfish through a tamis, or drum sieve. This is much simpler and the result is just as smooth.

INGREDIENTS

Serves 6–8

675g/1½lb small or medium cooked
    prawns in the shell
25ml/1½ tbsp vegetable oil
2 onions, halved and sliced
1 large carrot, sliced
2 celery sticks, sliced
2 litres/3⅓ pints/8 cups water
a few drops of lemon juice
30ml/2 tbsp tomato purée
bouquet garni
50g/2oz butter
50g/2oz plain flour
45–60ml/3–4 tbsp brandy
150ml/¼ pint/⅔ cup whipping cream
salt and freshly ground white pepper
flat leaf parsley sprig, to garnish

1 Remove the heads and peel away the shells from the prawns, reserving them for the stock. Chill the prawns.

2 Heat the oil in a large saucepan, add the prawn heads and shells and cook over a high heat, stirring frequently, until they start to brown. Reduce the heat to medium, add the onions, carrot and celery and fry gently, stirring occasionally, for about 5 minutes until the onions start to soften.

3 Add the water, lemon juice, tomato purée and bouquet garni. Bring the stock to the boil, then reduce the heat, cover and simmer gently for 25 minutes. Strain the stock through a sieve.

4 Melt the butter in a heavy saucepan over a medium heat. Stir in the flour and cook until just golden, stirring occasionally. Add the brandy and gradually pour in about half of the prawn stock, whisking vigorously until smooth, then whisk in the remaining liquid. Season to taste. Reduce the heat, cover and simmer for 5 minutes, stirring frequently.

5 Strain the soup into a clean saucepan. Add the cream and a little extra lemon juice to taste, if wished, then stir in most of the reserved prawns and cook over a medium heat until hot. Serve at once, garnished with the reserved prawns and parsley.

Mussel Bisque

Served hot, this makes a delicious and very filling soup, perfect for a light, lunch-time meal. It is also excellent cold.

INGREDIENTS

Serves 6

675g/1½lb fresh mussels in their shells
150ml/¼ pint/⅔ cup dry white wine or
   dry cider
475ml/16fl oz/2 cups water
25g/1oz butter
1 small red onion, chopped
1 small leek, thinly sliced
1 carrot, finely diced
2 tomatoes, skinned, seeded and chopped
2 garlic cloves, crushed
15ml/1 tbsp chopped fresh parsley
15ml/1 tbsp chopped fresh basil
1 celery stick, finely sliced
½ red pepper, seeded and chopped
250ml/8fl oz/1 cup whipping cream
salt and freshly ground black pepper

1 Scrub the mussels and pull off the beards. Discard any with broken shells or any that do not close when sharply tapped. Place them in a large pan with half the wine and 150ml/¼ pint/⅔ cup of the water.

2 Cover and cook the mussels over a high heat until they open up. (Discard any which do not open.) Transfer the mussels with a draining spoon to another dish and leave until cool enough to handle. Remove the mussels from their shells, leaving a few in their shells to garnish if you like.

3 Strain the cooking liquid through a clean piece of muslin or a fine cloth to remove any traces of sand or grit. Heat the butter in the same large pan and cook the onion, leek, carrot, tomatoes and garlic over a high heat for 2–3 minutes.

4 Reduce the heat and cook for a further 2–3 minutes, then add the cooking liquid, remaining water and wine, the parsley and basil and simmer for a further 10 minutes. Add the mussels, celery, red pepper, cream and seasoning to taste. Serve hot or cold.

Seafood Soup with Rouille

This is a really chunky, aromatic mixed fish soup from France, flavoured with plenty of saffron and herbs. Rouille, a fiery hot paste, is served separately for everyone to swirl into their soup to flavour.

INGREDIENTS

Serves 6

3 gurnard or red mullet, scaled and gutted
12 large raw or cooked prawns
675g/1½lb white fish, such as cod, haddock, halibut or monkfish
225g/8oz fresh mussels
1 onion, quartered
1.2 litres/2 pints/5 cups water
5ml/1 tsp saffron strands
15ml/1tbsp boiling water
75ml/5 tbsp olive oil
1 fennel bulb, roughly chopped
4 garlic cloves, crushed
3 strips orange rind
4 thyme sprigs
675g/1½lb tomatoes or 400g/14oz can chopped tomatoes
30ml/2 tbsp sun-dried tomato paste
3 bay leaves
salt and freshly ground black pepper

For the rouille
1 red pepper, seeded and roughly chopped
1 red chilli, seeded and sliced
2 garlic cloves, chopped
75ml/5 tbsp olive oil
15g/½oz fresh breadcrumbs

1 To make the rouille, process the pepper, chilli, garlic, oil and breadcrumbs in a blender or food processor until smooth. Transfer to a serving dish and chill.

2 Fillet the gurnard or mullet by cutting away the flesh from either side of the backbone, reserving the heads and bones. Cut the fillets into small chunks. Peel half the prawns and reserve the trimmings to make the stock. Skin the white fish, discarding any bones, and cut the flesh into large chunks. Scrub the mussels well, discarding any damaged ones and any that do not close immediately when tapped sharply with the back of a knife.

3 Put the fish trimmings and prawn trimmings in a saucepan with the onion and water. Bring to the boil, then simmer gently for 30 minutes. Cool slightly and strain.

4 Soak the saffron in the boiling water. Heat 30ml/2 tbsp of the olive oil in a large sauté pan or saucepan. Add the gurnard or mullet and white fish and fry over a high heat for 1 minute. Drain.

5 Heat the remaining oil and fry the fennel, garlic, orange rind and thyme until beginning to colour. Measure the strained stock and make up to about 1.2 litres/ 2 pints/5 cups with water.

6 If using fresh tomatoes, plunge them into boiling water for 30 seconds, then refresh in cold water. Skin and chop. Add the stock to the pan with the saffron, tomatoes, sun-dried tomato paste and bay leaves. Season to taste. Bring almost to the boil, lower the heat, then simmer gently, covered, for 20 minutes.

7 Stir in the gurnard or mullet, white fish and prawns, peeled and unpeeled, and add the mussels. Cover the pan and cook for 3–4 minutes. Discard any mussels that do not open. Serve the soup hot with the rouille.

COOK'S TIP

To save time, order the fish and ask the fishmonger to fillet the gurnard or mullet for you.

Spiced Mussel Soup

Chunky and colourful, this Turkish fish soup is similar to a chowder in its consistency. It is flavoured with harissa sauce, more familiar in North African cookery.

INGREDIENTS

Serves 6

1.5kg/3–3½lb fresh mussels
150ml/¼ pint/⅔ cup white wine
3 tomatoes
30ml/2 tbsp olive oil
1 onion, finely chopped
2 garlic cloves, crushed
2 celery sticks, thinly sliced
bunch of spring onions, thinly sliced
1 potato, diced
7.5ml/1½ tsp harissa sauce
45ml/3 tbsp chopped fresh parsley
freshly ground black pepper
thick yogurt, to serve

1 Scrub the mussels and remove the beards, discarding any with damaged shells or any open ones that do not close immediately when tapped sharply with a knife.

2 Bring the wine to the boil in a large saucepan. Add the mussels and cover with a lid. Cook for 4–5 minutes until the mussels have opened fully. Discard any mussels that remain closed. Drain the mussels, reserving the cooking liquid. Strain the cooking liquid through a clean piece of muslin or fine cloth to remove any traces of grit. Reserve a few of the mussels in their shells for garnish and shell the remainder.

3 Plunge the tomatoes into boiling water for 30 seconds, then refresh in cold water. Skin and dice them. Heat the olive oil in a heavy-based pan and fry the onion, garlic, celery and spring onions for 5 minutes.

4 Reserve a little of the onion mix. Add the shelled mussels, reserved liquid, potato, harissa sauce and tomatoes. Bring just to the boil, reduce the heat and cover. Simmer gently for 25 minutes, or until the potato is breaking up.

COOK'S TIP
Harissa is a spicy purée made from peppers, cayenne, olive oil, garlic, coriander, cumin and mint.

5 Stir in the parsley and pepper and add the reserved mussels. Heat through for 1 minute. Garnish with the reserved onion mix. Serve hot with a spoonful of yogurt.

Fish and Okra Soup

The inspiration for this soup came from a traditional Ghanaian recipe. Chop the okra to achieve a more authentic consistency.

Serves 4

2 green bananas
50g/2oz butter or margarine
1 onion, finely chopped
2 tomatoes, skinned and finely chopped
115g/4oz okra, trimmed
225g/8oz smoked haddock or cod fillet,
    cut into bite-sized pieces
900ml/1½ pints/3¾ cups fish stock
1 fresh chilli, seeded and chopped
salt and freshly ground black pepper
chopped fresh parsley, to garnish

3 Add the fish, fish stock, chilli and seasoning. Bring to the boil, then reduce the heat and simmer for about 20 minutes or until the fish is cooked through and flakes easily.

4 Peel the cooked bananas and cut into slices. Stir into the soup, heat through for a few minutes and then ladle into soup bowls. Sprinkle with the chopped parsley and serve.

1 Slit the skins of the green bananas, but do not peel. Place them in a large saucepan. Cover with water, bring to the boil and cook over a moderate heat for about 25 minutes, or until the bananas are tender. Transfer to a plate and leave to cool.

2 Melt the butter or margarine in a large saucepan and sauté the onion for about 5 minutes until soft. Stir in the chopped tomatoes and okra and fry gently for a further 10 minutes.

Noodle Soup with Pork and Szechuan Pickle

This soup is a meal in itself and the hot pickle gives it a delicious tang.

INGREDIENTS

Serves 4

1 litre/1¾ pints/4 cups chicken stock
350g/12oz egg noodles
15ml/1 tbsp dried prawns, soaked in water
30ml/2 tbsp vegetable oil
225g/8oz lean pork, finely shredded
15ml/1 tbsp yellow bean paste
15ml/1 tbsp soy sauce
115g/4oz Szechuan hot pickle, rinsed, drained and shredded
pinch of sugar
2 spring onions, finely sliced, to garnish

1 Bring the stock to the boil in a large saucepan. Add the noodles and cook until almost tender. Drain the dried prawns, rinse them under cold water, drain again and add to the stock. Lower the heat and simmer for a further 2 minutes. Keep hot.

2 Heat the oil in a frying pan or wok. Add the pork and stir-fry over a high heat for 3 minutes.

3 Add the bean paste and soy sauce to the pork; stir-fry for 1 minute more. Add the hot pickle with a pinch of sugar. Stir-fry for 1 minute more.

4 Divide the noodles and soup among individual serving bowls. Spoon the pork mixture on top, then sprinkle with the spring onions and serve at once.

Snapper and Noodle Soup

Tamarind gives this light, fragrant noodle soup a slightly sour taste.

INGREDIENTS

Serves 4

2 litres/3⅓ pints/8 cups water
1kg/2¼lb red snapper (or other red fish, such as mullet)
1 onion, sliced
50g/2oz tamarind pods
15ml/1 tbsp fish sauce
15ml/1 tbsp sugar
30ml/2 tbsp vegetable oil
2 garlic cloves, finely chopped
2 lemon grass stalks, very finely chopped
4 ripe tomatoes, roughly chopped
30ml/2 tbsp yellow bean paste
225g/8oz rice vermicelli, soaked in warm water until soft
115g/4oz beansprouts
8–10 basil or mint sprigs
25g/1oz roasted peanuts, ground
salt and freshly ground black pepper

1 Bring the water to the boil in a saucepan. Lower the heat and add the fish and onion, with 2.5ml/½ tsp salt. Simmer gently until the fish is cooked through.

2 Remove the fish from the stock; set aside. Add the tamarind, fish sauce and sugar to the stock. Cook for 5 minutes, then strain into a bowl. Carefully remove all the bones from the fish, keeping the flesh in big pieces.

3 Heat the oil in a large frying pan. Add the garlic and lemon grass and fry for a few seconds. Stir in the tomatoes and bean paste. Cook gently for 5–7 minutes, until the tomatoes are soft. Add the stock, bring back to a simmer and adjust the seasoning.

4 Drain the vermicelli. Plunge it into a saucepan of boiling water for a few minutes, drain and divide among individual serving bowls. Add the beansprouts, fish, basil or mint and sprinkle the ground peanuts on top. Top up each bowl with the hot soup.

Crab and Egg Noodle Broth

This delicious broth is the perfect solution when you are hungry, time is short, and you need something fast, nutritious and filling.

INGREDIENTS

Serves 4

75g/3oz fine egg noodles
25g/1oz unsalted butter
1 small bunch spring onions, chopped
1 celery stick, sliced
1 medium carrot, peeled and cut
    into batons
1.2 litres/2 pints/5 cups chicken stock
60ml/4 tbsp dry sherry
115g/4oz white crab meat, fresh or frozen
pinch of celery salt
pinch of cayenne pepper
10ml/2 tsp lemon juice
1 small bunch coriander or flat leaf
    parsley, to garnish

3 Add the chicken stock and sherry to the pan, bring to the boil, reduce the heat and simmer for a further 5 minutes.

4 If using frozen crab meat, allow it to thaw. Flake the crab meat between your fingers on to a plate and remove any stray pieces of shell.

5 Drain the noodles and add to the broth, together with the crab meat. Season to taste with celery salt and cayenne pepper and sharpen with the lemon juice. Return to a simmer.

6 Ladle the broth into shallow soup plates, scatter with roughly chopped coriander or parsley and serve.

1 Bring a large saucepan of water to the boil. Toss in the egg noodles and cook according to the instructions on the packet. Cool under cold running water and leave immersed in water until required.

2 Heat the butter in another large pan, add the spring onions, celery and carrot, cover and soften the vegetables over a gentle heat for 3–4 minutes.

Corn and Crab Meat Soup

This soup originated in the United States, but it has since been introduced into China. You must use creamed corn in the recipe to achieve the right consistency.

Serves 4

115g/4oz crab meat or chicken breast fillet
10ml/2 tsp finely chopped fresh
    root ginger
2 egg whites
30ml/2 tbsp milk
15ml/1 tbsp cornflour paste
600ml/1 pint/2½ cups vegetable or
    chicken stock
225g/8oz can creamed sweetcorn
salt and freshly ground black pepper
finely chopped spring onions, to garnish

1 Flake the crab meat (or roughly chop the chicken breast) and mix with the ginger.

2 Beat the egg whites until frothy, add the milk and cornflour paste and beat again until smooth. Blend with the crab meat or chicken breast.

3 In a wok or saucepan, bring the stock to the boil, add the creamed sweetcorn and bring back to the boil.

4 Stir in the crab meat or chicken breast and egg-white mixture, adjust the seasonings and stir gently until well blended and the meat is cooked. Serve garnished with finely chopped spring onions.

Main Course Spicy Shrimp and Noodle Soup

This dish is served as a hot coconut broth with a separate platter of prawns, fish and noodles. Diners are invited to add their own choice of accompaniments to the broth.

INGREDIENTS

Serves 4–6

25g/1oz shelled, raw cashew nuts

3 shallots, or 1 medium onion, sliced

5cm/2in piece lemon grass, shredded

2 garlic cloves, crushed

150g/5oz spaghetti-size rice noodles, soaked for 10 minutes

30ml/2 tbsp vegetable oil

1cm/½in square piece shrimp paste, or 15ml/1 tbsp fish sauce

15ml/1 tbsp mild curry paste

400g/14oz can coconut milk

½ chicken stock cube

3 curry leaves (optional)

450g/1lb white fish fillet, such as cod, haddock or whiting

225g/8oz raw or cooked prawn tails

1 small lettuce, shredded

115g/4oz beansprouts

3 spring onions, shredded

½ cucumber, sliced and shredded

prawn crackers, to serve

1 Grind the cashew nuts using a pestle and mortar or in a food processor with the shallots or onion, lemon grass and garlic. Cook the noodles according to the packet instructions.

3 Add the shrimp paste or fish sauce and curry paste, followed by the coconut milk, stock cube and curry leaves. Mix thoroughly and simmer for 10 minutes.

2 Heat the oil in a large wok or saucepan, add the contents of the mortar or food processor, and fry for about 1–2 minutes, or until the nuts begin to brown.

4 Cut the white fish into bite-sized pieces. Place the fish and prawn tails in a large frying basket, immerse in the simmering coconut stock, and cook for 3–4 minutes. Transfer the fish and prawn tails to a serving platter with the salad and noodles and transfer the broth to a tureen or lidded pot and serve (see Cook's Tip).

COOK'S TIP

To serve, line a large serving platter with the shredded lettuce leaves. Arrange the beansprouts, spring onions and cucumber in neat piles, together with the cooked fish, prawns and noodles. Serve the salad with a bowl of prawn crackers and the broth in a lidded stoneware pot.

STARTERS

Olive and Anchovy Bites

These melt-in-the-mouth morsels store very well; freeze them for up to 3 months or they can be kept in an airtight container for up to 2 weeks before serving.

Makes 40–45

115g/4oz plain flour
115g/4oz chilled butter
115g/4oz finely grated cheese, such as
   Manchego, mature Cheddar or Gruyère
50g/2oz can anchovy fillets in oil, drained
   and roughly chopped
50g/2oz stoned black olives,
   roughly chopped
2.5ml/½ tsp cayenne pepper
sea salt

1 Place the flour, butter, cheese, anchovies, olives and cayenne in a food processor and pulse until the mixture forms a firm dough.

2 Wrap the dough loosely in clear film. Set aside in the refrigerator to chill for 20 minutes.

3 Unwrap the dough and turn it out on to a lightly floured surface. Knead lightly and roll it out thinly.

4 Cut the dough into 5cm/2in wide strips, then cut across each strip diagonally, in alternate directions, to make triangles. Transfer to baking sheets and bake in a preheated oven at 200°C/ 400°F/Gas 6 for 8–10 minutes, until golden. Cool on a wire rack. Sprinkle generously with sea salt before serving.

COOK'S TIP

For a change, sprinkle the olive and anchovy bites with finely grated Parmesan cheese or dust lightly with cayenne pepper before baking.

Smoked Salmon Pancakes with Pesto

These simple pancakes take no more than 10–15 minutes to prepare and are perfect for a special occasion. Smoked salmon is delicious with fresh basil and combines well with toasted pine nuts and a spoonful of crème fraîche.

INGREDIENTS

Makes 12–16

120ml/4fl oz/½ cup milk
115g/4oz self-raising flour
1 egg
30ml/2 tbsp pesto sauce
vegetable oil, for frying
200ml/7fl oz/scant 1 cup crème fraîche
75g/3oz smoked salmon
15g/½oz pine nuts, toasted
salt and freshly ground black pepper
12–16 fresh basil sprigs, to garnish

3 Heat the vegetable oil in a large frying pan. Spoon the pancake mixture into the heated oil in small heaps. Allow about 30 seconds for the pancakes to rise, then turn and cook briefly on the other side. Keep warm. Continue cooking the pancakes in batches until all the batter has been used up.

4 Arrange the pancakes on a serving plate and top each one with a spoonful of crème fraîche.

5 Cut the salmon into 1cm/½ in strips and place on top of each pancake. Scatter each pancake with pine nuts and garnish with a sprig of fresh basil.

1 Pour half of the milk into a mixing bowl. Add the flour, egg, pesto sauce and seasoning and mix to a smooth batter.

2 Add the remainder of the milk and stir until evenly blended.

Seafood Pancakes

The combination of fresh and smoked haddock imparts a wonderful flavour to the filling.

INGREDIENTS

Serves 4–6
For the pancakes
115g/4oz plain flour
pinch of salt
1 egg, plus 1 egg yolk
300ml/½ pint/1¼ cups milk
15ml/1 tbsp melted butter, plus extra for
    cooking
50–75g/2–3oz Gruyère cheese, grated
curly salad leaves, to serve

For the filling
225g/8oz smoked haddock fillet
225g/8oz fresh haddock fillet
300ml/½ pint/1¼ cups milk
150ml/¼ pint/⅔ cup single cream
40g/1½oz butter
40g/1½oz plain flour
freshly grated nutmeg
2 hard-boiled eggs, shelled and chopped
salt and freshly ground black pepper

1 To make the pancakes, sift the flour and salt into a bowl. Make a well in the centre and add the egg and egg yolk. Whisk the eggs, starting to incorporate some of the flour from around the edges.

2 Gradually add the milk, whisking all the time, until the batter is smooth and has the consistency of thin cream. Stir in the melted butter.

3 Heat a small crêpe pan or omelette pan until hot, then rub round the inside of the pan with a pad of kitchen paper dipped in melted butter.

4 Pour about 30ml/2 tbsp of the batter into the pan, then tip the pan to coat the base evenly. Cook for about 30 seconds until the underside of the pancake is golden brown.

5 Flip the pancake over and cook the other side until lightly browned. Repeat to make 12 pancakes, rubbing the pan with melted butter between cooking each pancake. Stack the pancakes as you make them between sheets of greaseproof paper. Keep warm on a plate set over a pan of simmering water.

6 Put the smoked and fresh haddock fillets in a large pan. Add the milk and poach for 6–8 minutes, until just tender. Lift out the fish using a slotted spoon and, when cool enough to handle, remove the skin and any bones. Reserve the milk.

7 Pour the single cream into a measuring jug, then strain enough of the reserved milk into the jug to make the quantity up to 450ml/¾ pint/1⅞ cups.

8 Melt the butter in a pan, stir in the flour and cook gently for 1 minute. Gradually mix in the milk mixture, stirring continuously, to make a smooth sauce. Cook for 2–3 minutes, until thickened. Season with salt, pepper and nutmeg. Roughly flake the haddock and fold into the sauce with the eggs. Leave to cool.

9 Divide the filling among the pancakes. Fold the sides of each pancake into the centre, then roll them up so that the filling is completely enclosed.

10 Butter four or six individual ovenproof dishes and arrange 2–3 filled pancakes in each, or butter one large dish for all the pancakes. Brush with melted butter and cook in a preheated oven at 180°C/350°F/ Gas 4 for 15 minutes. Sprinkle over the Gruyère and cook for a further 5 minutes, until warmed through. Serve hot with a few curly salad leaves.

VARIATION

To ring the changes, add cooked, peeled prawns, smoked mussels or cooked fresh, shelled mussels to the filling, instead of the chopped hard-boiled eggs.

Sautéed Scallops

Scallops go well with all sorts of sauces, but simple cooking is the best way to enjoy their flavour.

INGREDIENTS

Serves 4

450g/1lb shelled scallops
25g/1oz butter
30ml/2 tbsp dry white vermouth
15ml/1 tbsp finely chopped fresh parsley
salt and freshly ground black pepper

1 Rinse the scallops under cold running water to remove any sand or grit and pat dry using kitchen paper. Season them lightly with salt and pepper.

2 In a frying pan large enough to hold the scallops in one layer, heat half the butter until it begins to colour. Sauté the scallops for 3–5 minutes, turning, until golden brown on both sides and just firm to the touch. Remove to a serving platter and cover to keep warm.

3 Add the vermouth to the hot frying pan, swirl in the remaining butter, add the parsley and pour the sauce over the scallops. Serve immediately.

Garlicky Scallops and Prawns

Scallops and prawns are found all along the Atlantic and Mediterranean coasts of France and are enjoyed in every region. This method of cooking is a typical Provençal recipe.

INGREDIENTS

Serves 2–4

6 large shelled scallops
6–8 large raw prawns, peeled
plain flour, for dusting
30–45ml/2–3 tbsp olive oil
1 garlic clove, finely chopped
15ml/1 tbsp chopped fresh basil
30–45ml/2–3 tbsp lemon juice
salt and freshly ground black pepper

1 Rinse the scallops under cold running water to remove any sand or grit. Pat them dry using kitchen paper and cut in half crossways. Season the scallops and prawns with salt and pepper and dust lightly with flour, shaking off the excess.

2 Heat the oil in a large frying pan over a high heat and add the scallops and prawns.

3 Reduce the heat to medium-high and cook for 2 minutes, then turn the scallops and prawns. Add the garlic and basil, shaking the pan to distribute them evenly. Cook for a further 2 minutes until the scallops are golden and just firm to the touch. Sprinkle over the lemon juice and toss to blend.

VARIATION

To make a richer sauce, transfer the cooked scallops and prawns to a warmed plate. Pour 60ml/4 tbsp dry white wine into the frying pan and boil to reduce by half. Add 15g/½oz unsalted butter, whisking until it melts and the sauce thickens slightly. Pour over the scallops and prawns and serve.

Scallops Wrapped in Parma Ham

This is a delicious summer recipe for cooking over the barbecue.

INGREDIENTS

Serves 4

24 medium-size scallops, without corals,
    prepared for cooking
lemon juice
8–12 slices Parma ham
olive oil
freshly ground black pepper
lemon wedges, to serve

1 Preheat the grill or prepare a charcoal fire. Sprinkle the scallops with lemon juice. Cut the Parma ham into long strips. Wrap one strip around each scallop. Thread them on to 8 skewers.

2 Brush with oil. Arrange on a baking sheet if grilling. Cook about 10cm/4in from the heat under a preheated grill for 3–5 minutes on each side or until the scallops are opaque and tender. Alternatively, cook over charcoal, turning once, until the scallops are opaque and tender.

3 Set 2 skewers on each plate. Sprinkle the scallops with freshly ground black pepper and serve with lemon wedges.

COOK'S TIP

The edible parts of the scallop are the round white muscle and the coral or roe. When preparing fresh scallops, keep the skirt – the frilly part – for making stock.

Mussels Steamed in White Wine

*This is the best and easiest way to
serve the small tender mussels,
bouchots, which are farmed along
much of the French coast line. Serve
with plenty of crusty French bread
to dip in the juices.*

INGREDIENTS

Serves 4

1.75kg/4–4½lb mussels

300ml/½ pint/1¼ cups dry white wine

4–6 large shallots, finely chopped

bouquet garni

freshly ground black pepper

1 Discard any broken mussels
and those with open shells that
do not close immediately when
tapped sharply. Under cold
running water, scrape the mussel
shells with a knife to remove any
barnacles and pull out the stringy
'beards'. Soak the mussels in
several changes of cold water for at
least 1 hour.

2 In a large, heavy, flameproof
casserole combine the white
wine, shallots, bouquet garni and
plenty of pepper. Bring to the boil
over a medium-high heat and cook
for 2 minutes.

3 Add the mussels to the
casserole, cover tightly and
cook, shaking and tossing the pan
occasionally, for 5 minutes, or until
the mussels have opened. Discard
any mussels that have not opened.

4 Using a slotted spoon, divide
the mussels among 4 warmed
soup plates. Tilt the casserole a
little and hold for a few seconds to
allow any sand to sink to the
bottom and settle. Alternatively,
strain the cooking liquid through
clean muslin.

5 Spoon or pour the cooking
liquid over the mussels and
serve at once.

VARIATION

For Mussels with Cream Sauce,
cook the shellfish as described
here, but transfer the mussels to a
warmed bowl and cover to keep
warm. Strain the cooking liquid
through a muslin-lined sieve into a
large saucepan and boil for about
7–10 minutes to reduce by half.
Stir in 90ml/6 tbsp whipping
cream and 30ml/2 tbsp chopped
fresh parsley, then add the mussels.
Cook for about 1 minute more to
reheat the mussels.

Grilled Sardines

Fresh sardines have plenty of flavour, so they are at their best when cooked simply.

INGREDIENTS

Serves 4

8 sardines, about 50g/2oz each
sea salt
2 lemons, halved, to serve

1 Gut the sardines, but leave on the heads and tails. With a sharp knife, slash each side of all the sardines diagonally three times.

2 Place the sardines on a grill rack and sprinkle with sea salt. Cook under a preheated high grill for 4 minutes on each side until the flesh is cooked and the skin is blistered and a little charred.

3 Transfer to a serving dish and serve at once with the lemon halves to squeeze over.

Salt-cured Salmon

This delicious treatment is a good alternative to smoked salmon.

INGREDIENTS

Serves 10

50g/2oz sea salt
45ml/3 tbsp caster sugar
5ml/1 tsp chilli powder
5ml/1 tsp freshly ground black pepper
45ml/3 tbsp chopped fresh coriander
2 salmon fillets, about 250g/9oz each
flat leaf parsley, to garnish
garlic mayonnaise, to serve

1 In a bowl, mix together the salt, sugar, chilli powder, pepper and coriander. Rub the mixture into the flesh of each salmon fillet.

2 Place one of the fillets, skin side down, in a shallow glass dish. Place the other fillet on top, with the skin side up. Cover with foil, then place a weight on top.

3 Chill for 48 hours, turning the fish every 8 hours or so and basting it with the liquid that forms in the dish.

4 Drain the salmon well and transfer to a board. Using a sharp knife, slice it diagonally into wafer-thin slices. Arrange on plates and garnish with sprigs of parsley. Serve with garlic mayonnaise.

COOK'S TIP

Make the most of the leftover salmon skin by turning it into delicious crunchy strips: after slicing the salt-cured salmon, scrape any remaining fish off the skin and discard. Cut the skin into 1cm/½in wide strips. Fry for 1 minute in hot oil until crisp and browned. Drain on kitchen paper and allow to cool. Serve as a garnish for the salt-cured salmon or as a tapas dish in its own right.

Deep-fried Whitebait

A spicy coating on these fish gives this favourite dish a crunchy bite.

INGREDIENTS

Serves 6

115g/4oz plain flour

2.5ml/½ tsp curry powder

2.5ml/½ tsp ground ginger

2.5ml/½ tsp ground cayenne pepper

pinch of salt

1.1kg/2½lb fresh or frozen
   whitebait, thawed

vegetable oil for deep-frying

lemon wedges, to garnish

1 Mix together the flour, spices and salt in a large bowl.

2 Coat the fish in the seasoned flour and shake off any excess.

3 Heat the oil in a large, heavy-based saucepan until it reaches a temperature of 190°C/375°F. Fry the whitebait in batches for about 2–3 minutes until the fish is golden and crispy.

4 Drain well on absorbent kitchen paper. Serve hot, garnished with lemon wedges.

Sesame Prawn Toasts

Serve about four triangles each with a soy sauce dip.

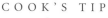

INGREDIENTS

Serves 6

175g/6oz cooked prawns, peeled
   and deveined
2 spring onions, finely chopped
2.5cm/1in fresh root ginger, grated
2 garlic cloves, crushed
25g/1oz cornflour
10ml/2 tsp soy sauce, plus extra
   for dipping
6 slices stale bread from a small loaf,
   crusts removed
40g/1½oz sesame seeds
vegetable oil for deep-frying

1 Place the prawns, spring onions, ginger and garlic cloves into a food processor fitted with a metal blade. Add the cornflour and soy sauce and work the ingredients into a thick paste.

2 Spread the bread slices evenly with the paste and sprinkle with the sesame seeds, making sure that they stick to the bread. Cut the slices into triangles and chill in the refrigerator for 30 minutes.

3 Heat the oil for deep-frying in a large, heavy-based pan until it reaches a temperature of 190°C/375°F. Using a slotted spoon, lower half the toasts into the oil, sesame seed side down, and fry for about 2–3 minutes, turning over for the last minute. Drain on absorbent kitchen paper. Keep the toasts warm while frying the remainder.

4 Serve the toasts with the soy sauce for dipping.

COOK'S TIP
~
If you do not have a deep-fat thermometer, check that the oil is at the right temperature by tossing a stale bread cube into it. If it turns golden in 30 seconds, the temperature is just right.

Monkfish Parcels

These little dumplings of spiced fish taste delicious with the dressing of tomato oil.

Serves 4

175g/6oz strong plain flour
2 eggs
115g/4oz skinless monkfish fillet, diced
grated rind of 1 lemon
1 garlic clove, chopped
1 small, fresh, red chilli, seeded and sliced
45ml/3 tbsp chopped fresh parsley
30ml/2 tbsp single cream
flour, for dusting
salt and freshly ground black pepper

For the tomato oil

2 tomatoes, skinned, seeded and
    finely diced
45ml/3 tbsp extra virgin olive oil
30ml/2 tbsp fresh lemon juice

1 Place the flour, eggs and 2.5ml/½ tsp salt in a food processor; pulse until the mixture forms a soft dough. Knead gently for 2–3 minutes until smooth, then wrap in clear film. Chill in the refrigerator for 20 minutes.

2 Place the monkfish, lemon rind, garlic, chilli and parsley in the clean food processor and process until very finely chopped. Add the cream, with plenty of salt and pepper and work again to form a very thick purée.

3 Make the tomato oil by stirring the diced tomato with the olive oil and lemon juice in a bowl. Add salt to taste. Cover and chill.

4 Roll out the dough on a lightly floured surface and cut out 32 rounds, using a 4cm/1½in plain cutter. Divide the filling among half the rounds, then cover with the remaining rounds. Pinch the edges tightly to seal, excluding as much air as possible.

5 Bring a large saucepan of water to simmering point and poach the parcels, in batches, for 2–3 minutes, or until they rise to the surface. Drain and serve hot, drizzled with the tomato oil.

Crab and Ricotta Tartlets

Use the meat from a freshly cooked crab, weighing about 450g/1lb, if you can. Otherwise, look out for frozen brown and white crab meat.

INGREDIENTS

Serves 4

225g/8oz plain flour
115g/4oz butter, diced
about 60ml/4 tbsp iced water
225g/8oz ricotta
15ml/1 tbsp grated onion
30ml/2 tbsp grated Parmesan cheese
2.5ml/½ tsp mustard powder
2 eggs, plus 1 egg yolk
225g/8oz crab meat
30ml/2 tbsp chopped fresh parsley
2.5–5ml/½–1 tsp anchovy essence
5–10ml/1–2 tsp lemon juice
salt and cayenne pepper
salad leaves, to garnish

1 Sift the flour and a good pinch of salt into a mixing bowl, add the diced butter and rub it in with your fingertips, until the mixture resembles fine breadcrumbs. Gradually stir in enough iced water to make a firm dough.

2 Turn the dough on to a floured surface and knead lightly. Roll out the pastry and use to line four 10cm/4in tartlet tins. Prick the bases with a fork, then chill in the refrigerator for 30 minutes.

3 Line the pastry cases with greaseproof paper and fill with baking beans. Bake in a preheated oven at 200°C/400°F/Gas 6 for 10 minutes, then remove the paper and beans. Return to the oven and bake for a further 10 minutes.

4 Place the ricotta, grated onion, Parmesan and mustard in a bowl and beat until soft. Gradually beat in the eggs and egg yolk.

5 Gently stir in the crab meat and chopped parsley, then add the anchovy essence, lemon juice, salt and cayenne pepper, to taste.

6 Remove the tartlet cases from the oven and reduce the temperature to 180°C/350°F/Gas 4. Spoon the filling into the cases and bake for 20 minutes, until set and golden brown. Serve hot with a garnish of salad leaves.

Crab Savoury

This scrumptious, baked seafood dish is rich and creamy.

INGREDIENTS

Serves 4

25g/1oz butter
1 small onion, finely chopped
50g/2oz fresh brown breadcrumbs
225g/8oz crab meat
150ml/¼ pint/⅔ cup soured cream
10–15ml/2–3 tsp prepared mustard
pinch of cayenne pepper
squeeze of lemon juice
75ml/5 tbsp finely grated Cheddar cheese
salt

1 Melt the butter in a saucepan over a medium heat, then cook the onion gently for 2–3 minutes, until it is soft but not brown.

2 Stir the breadcrumbs, crab meat, soured cream and prepared mustard into the onions. Add a generous sprinkling of cayenne pepper, lemon juice and salt to taste. Heat through gently, stirring carefully.

3 Spoon the crab mixture into a baking dish, sprinkle the grated cheese over the top and place under a preheated, hot grill until golden and bubbling.

Smoked Mackerel Pâté

The pâté can be flavoured with horseradish, if liked.

INGREDIENTS

Serves 4

275g/10oz smoked mackerel fillet, skinned
90ml/6 tbsp soured cream
75g/3oz unsalted butter, softened
30ml/2 tbsp chopped fresh parsley
15–30ml/1–2 tbsp lemon juice
freshly ground black pepper
chicory leaves and parsley, to garnish
fingers of toast, to serve

1 Remove any fine bones from the mackerel fillet, then mash it with a fork.

2 Work the soured cream and butter into the mackerel until smooth. Stir in the parsley and add lemon juice and pepper to taste.

3 Pack the mackerel mixture into a dish or bowl, then cover tightly and chill in the refrigerator for 6–8 hours or overnight.

4 About 30 minutes before serving, remove the pâté from the refrigerator to allow it to return to room temperature. To serve, spoon on to individual plates and garnish with chicory leaves and parsley. Serve with fingers of toast.

COOK'S TIP

For a less rich (and lower-calorie) version of this pâté, substitute 200g/7oz low-fat soft cheese or sieved cottage cheese for the soured cream.

Sole Goujons with Lime Mayonnaise

This simple dish can be rustled up very quickly. It also makes an excellent light lunch or supper.

INGREDIENTS

Serves 4

200ml/7fl oz/scant 1 cup mayonnaise
1 small garlic clove, crushed
10ml/2 tsp capers, rinsed and chopped
10ml/2 tsp chopped gherkins
grated rind and juice of 1 lime
15ml/1 tbsp finely chopped
   fresh coriander
675g/1½lb sole fillets, skinned
2 eggs, beaten
115g/4oz/2 cups fresh white breadcrumbs
oil, for deep-frying
salt and freshly ground black pepper
lime wedges, to serve

1 To make the lime mayonnaise, mix together the mayonnaise, garlic, capers, gherkins, lime rind and juice and chopped coriander. Season with salt and pepper to taste. Transfer to a serving bowl and chill until required.

2 Cut the sole fillets into finger-length strips. Dip each strip first into the beaten egg, then into the breadcrumbs.

3 Heat the oil in a deep-fat fryer to 180°C/350°F. Add the fish strips, in batches, and fry until they are golden brown and crisp. Drain well on kitchen paper and keep warm while you cook the remaining strips.

4 Pile the goujons on to warmed serving plates and serve with the lime wedges for squeezing over. Hand the sauce round separately.

Spicy Fish Rösti

You can also serve these fish cakes crisp and hot for lunch or supper with a mixed green salad.

INGREDIENTS

Serves 4

350g/12oz large, firm waxy potatoes
350g/12oz salmon or cod fillet, skinned
   and boned
3–4 spring onions, finely chopped
5ml/1 tsp grated fresh root ginger
30ml/2 tbsp chopped fresh coriander
10ml/2 tsp lemon juice
30–45ml/2–3 tbsp sunflower oil
salt and cayenne pepper
coriander sprigs, to garnish
lemon wedges, to serve

1 Cook the potatoes with their skins on in a pan of boiling salted water for 10 minutes. Drain and leave to cool for a few minutes.

2 Meanwhile, finely chop the salmon or cod fillet and put into a bowl. Stir in the chopped spring onions, grated root ginger, chopped coriander and lemon juice. Season to taste with salt and cayenne pepper.

3 When the potatoes are cool enough to handle, peel off the skins and grate the potatoes coarsely. Gently stir the grated potato into the fish mixture.

4 Form the fish mixture into 12 cakes, pressing the mixture together and leaving the edges slightly rough.

5 Heat the oil in a large frying pan and fry the fish cakes, a few at a time, for 3 minutes on each side, until golden brown and crisp. Drain on kitchen paper. Serve hot, garnished with sprigs of coriander and with lemon wedges for squeezing over.

Ceviche

This makes an excellent starter. With the addition of sliced avocado, it could make a light summer lunch.

INGREDIENTS

Serves 6

450g/1lb mackerel fillets, cut into
    1cm/½in pieces
350ml/12fl oz/1½ cups freshly squeezed
    lime or lemon juice
225g/8oz tomatoes, chopped
1 small onion, very finely chopped
2 drained canned jalapeño chillies or
    4 serrano chillies, rinsed and chopped
60ml/4 tbsp olive oil
2.5ml/½ tsp dried oregano
30ml/2 tbsp chopped fresh coriander
salt and freshly ground black pepper
lemon wedges and fresh coriander,
    to garnish
stuffed green olives sprinkled with
    chopped coriander, to serve

1 Put the fish into a glass dish and pour over the lime or lemon juice, making sure that the fish is completely covered. Cover and chill for 6 hours, turning once, by which time the fish will be opaque, 'cooked' by the juice.

2 When the fish is opaque, lift it out of the juice and set it aside.

3 Combine the tomatoes, onion, chillies, olive oil, oregano and coriander in a bowl. Add salt and pepper to taste, then pour in the reserved juice from the mackerel. Mix well and pour over the fish.

4 Cover the dish and return the ceviche to the refrigerator for about 1 hour to allow the flavours to blend. Ceviche should not be served too cold. Allow it to stand at room temperature for 15 minutes before serving. Garnish with lemon wedges and coriander sprigs, and serve with stuffed olives sprinkled with chopped coriander.

COOK'S TIP

For a more delicately flavoured ceviche, you can use a white fish, such as sole.

Glazed Garlic Prawns

*This is a fairly simple and quick dish
to prepare. It is best to peel the
prawns, as this helps them to absorb
maximum flavour. Serve with a
salad as an appetizer or as a main
course with a selection of vegetables
and other accompaniments.*

INGREDIENTS

Serves 4

15ml/1 tbsp vegetable oil

3 garlic cloves, roughly chopped

3 tomatoes, chopped

2.5ml/½ tsp salt

5ml/1 tsp crushed dried red chillies

5ml/1 tsp lemon juice

15ml/1 tbsp mango chutney

1 fresh green chilli, chopped

15–20 cooked king prawns, peeled
  and deveined

fresh coriander sprigs, 4 unpeeled, cooked
  king prawns (optional) and 2 spring
  onions, chopped (optional), to garnish

1 In a medium saucepan, heat
the oil and add the chopped
garlic cloves.

2 Lower the heat and add the
chopped tomatoes along with
the salt, crushed chillies, lemon
juice, mango chutney and chopped
fresh chilli.

3 Finally, add the prawns, turn
up the heat and stir-fry them
quickly, until heated through.

4 Transfer to a warmed serving
dish. Serve garnished with
fresh coriander, unpeeled king
prawns and chopped spring
onions, if liked.

COOK'S TIP

This is a very fiery dish – if you
would prefer it less hot, carefully
seed the chilli before chopping
and reduce the crushed chillies
to a pinch.

Smoked Salmon Terrine with Lemons

Lemons can be cut and sliced in so many ways. This melt-in-the-mouth smoked salmon terrine gives a time-honoured accompaniment an intriguing new twist.

Serves 6

4 sheets of leaf gelatine
60ml/4 tbsp water
400g/14oz smoked salmon, sliced
300g/11oz/1½ cups cream cheese
120ml/4fl oz/½ cup crème fraîche
30ml/2 tbsp dill mustard
juice of 1 lime

For the garnish
2 lemons
piece of muslin
raffia, for tying

2 Set aside enough of the remaining smoked salmon to make a middle layer the length of the tin. Chop the rest finely by hand or in a food processor. Beat together the cream cheese, crème fraîche and dill mustard with the chopped smoked salmon until everything is well combined.

4 Tap the tin on the work surface to expel any trapped air. Fold over the overhanging salmon slices to cover the top. Cover with clear film and chill for at least 4 hours.

5 Make the garnish. Cut 1 lemon in half widthways. Wrap each half in a small square of muslin. Gather the muslin at the rounded end of the lemon and tie neatly with raffia.

1 Soak the gelatine in the water in a small bowl until softened. Meanwhile, line a 450g/1lb loaf tin with clear film. Use some of the smoked salmon to line the tin, laying the slices widthways across the base and up the sides and leaving enough overlap to fold over the top of the filling.

3 Squeeze out the gelatine and melt gently in a small saucepan with the lime juice. Add to the smoked salmon mixture and mix thoroughly. Spoon half the mixture into the lined tin. Lay the reserved smoked salmon slices on the mixture along the length of the tin, then spoon on the rest of the filling and smooth the top.

6 Cut a small 'V' from the side of the other lemon. Repeat at 5mm/¼in intervals. Turn out the terrine, then slice. Garnish with muslin-wrapped lemons and lemon 'leaves'.

Char-grilled Squid

Enjoy these tender bites of succulent squid right off the barbecue.

INGREDIENTS

Serves 4

1kg/2¼lb prepared squid
90ml/6 tbsp olive oil
juice of 1–2 lemons
3 garlic cloves, crushed
1.5ml/¼ tsp chilli flakes
60ml/4 tbsp chopped fresh parsley
lemon slices, to garnish

1 Reserve the squid tentacles, then, using a small, sharp knife, score the flesh into a diagonal pattern.

2 Place all the squid in a shallow, non-metallic dish. To make the marinade, thoroughly mix together the olive oil, lemon juice, crushed garlic and chilli flakes in a small bowl.

3 Pour the marinade over the squid and set aside in a cool place for a minimum of 2 hours, stirring occasionally.

4 Lift the squid from the dish and reserve the marinade. Cook the squid on a barbecue for 2 minutes on each side, turning them frequently and brushing with the marinade until the outside is golden brown and crisp, with soft, moist flesh inside.

5 Bring the remaining marinade to the boil in a small pan, stir in the chopped parsley, then pour over the squid. Garnish with lemon slices and serve at once.

Monkfish Brochettes

These brochettes are colourful as well as full of flavour.

INGREDIENTS

Serves 4

675g/1½lb monkfish, skinned and boned
12 rashers streaky bacon, rinded
2 small courgettes
1 yellow or orange pepper, seeded and cut
   into 2.5cm/1 in cubes
saffron rice, to serve

For the marinade
90ml/6 tbsp olive oil
grated rind of ½ lime
45ml/3 tbsp lime juice
30ml/2 tbsp dry white wine
60ml/4 tbsp chopped fresh mixed herbs,
   such as dill, chives and parsley
5ml/1 tsp clear honey
freshly ground black pepper

1 To make the marinade, mix together the olive oil, lime rind and juice, wine, chopped herbs, honey and pepper in a bowl, then set aside.

2 Cut the monkfish into 24 x 2.5cm/1 in cubes. Stretch the bacon rashers with the back of a knife, then cut each one in half and wrap around the monkfish cubes.

3 Pare strips of peel from the courgettes to give a stripy effect, then cut into 2.5cm/1 in chunks.

4 Thread the fish rolls on to skewers alternately with the courgettes and pepper. Place in a dish. Pour over the marinade and leave in a cool place for 1 hour. Lift out the skewers, then grill for about 10 minutes, turning and basting occasionally with the marinade. Serve with saffron rice.

COOK'S TIP

If you are using wooden skewers, soak them in cold water before threading the fish and vegetables, so that they do not char when the brochettes are cooking.

Thai Fish Cakes

Bursting with the flavour of chillies and lime, these little fish cakes make a wonderful starter.

INGREDIENTS

Serves 4

450g/1lb firm white fish fillets, such as cod or haddock

3 spring onions, sliced

30ml/2 tbsp chopped fresh coriander

30ml/2 tbsp Thai red curry paste

1 fresh green chilli, seeded and chopped

10ml/2 tsp grated lime rind

15ml/1 tbsp lime juice

30ml/2 tbsp groundnut oil

salt

crisp lettuce leaves, shredded, spring onions, fresh red chilli slices, coriander sprigs and lime wedges, to serve

1 Cut the fish into chunks about 2.5cm/1in, then place in a blender or food processor.

2 Add the spring onions, coriander, red curry paste, green chilli, lime rind and juice to the fish. Season with salt to taste. Process until finely minced.

3 Using lightly floured hands, divide the fish mixture into 16 pieces and shape each one into a small cake about 4cm/1½in across. Place the fish cakes on a plate, cover with clear film and chill in the refrigerator for about 2 hours until firm. Heat a wok over a high heat until hot. Add the oil and swirl it around.

4 Fry the fish cakes, a few at a time, for 6–8 minutes, turning them carefully, until they are evenly browned. Drain each batch on kitchen paper and keep hot while you are cooking the remainder. Serve on a bed of crisp lettuce leaves with shredded spring onions, red chilli slices, coriander sprigs and lime wedges.

Seafood Wontons with Coriander Dressing

These tasty wontons resemble tortellini. Water chestnuts add a light crunch to the filling.

INGREDIENTS

Serves 4

225g/8oz cooked prawns, peeled
   and deveined
115g/4oz white crab meat
4 canned water chestnuts, finely diced
1 spring onion, finely chopped
1 small green chilli, seeded and
   finely chopped
1.5ml/¼ tsp grated fresh root ginger
1 egg, separated
20–24 wonton wrappers
salt and freshly ground black pepper
coriander leaves, to garnish

For the coriander dressing
30ml/2 tbsp rice vinegar
15ml/1 tbsp chopped, pickled ginger
90ml/6 tbsp olive oil
15ml/1 tbsp soy sauce
45ml/3 tbsp chopped coriander
30ml/2 tbsp finely diced red pepper

1 Finely dice the prawns and place them in a bowl. Add the crab meat, water chestnuts, spring onion, chilli, ginger and egg white. Season with salt and pepper to taste and stir well.

2 Place a wonton wrapper on a board. Put about 5ml/1 tsp of the filling just above the centre of the wrapper. With a pastry brush, moisten the edges of the wrapper with a little of the egg yolk. Bring the bottom of the wrapper up over the filling. Press gently to expel any air, then seal the wrapper neatly in a triangle.

3 For a more elaborate shape, bring the two side points up over the filling, overlap the points and pinch the ends firmly together. Space the filled wontons on a large baking sheet lined with grease-proof paper, so that they do not stick together.

4 Half fill a large saucepan with water. Bring to simmering point. Add the filled wontons, a few at a time, and simmer for about 2–3 minutes, or until the wontons float to the surface. When ready, the wrappers will be translucent and the filling should be cooked. Remove the wontons with a large slotted spoon, drain them briefly, then spread them on trays. Keep warm while you cook the remaining wontons.

5 Make the coriander dressing by whisking all the ingredients together in a bowl. Divide the wontons among serving dishes, drizzle with the dressing and serve, garnished with a handful of coriander leaves.

Grilled Green Mussels with Cumin

Green-shelled mussels have a more distinctive flavour than the small, black variety. Keep the empty shells to use as individual salt and pepper holders for fishy meals.

Serves 4

45ml/3 tbsp fresh parsley
45ml/3 tbsp fresh coriander
1 garlic clove, crushed
pinch of ground cumin
25g/1oz unsalted butter, softened
25g/1oz brown breadcrumbs
12 green mussels or 24 small mussels, on
　the half-shell
freshly ground black pepper
chopped fresh parsley, to garnish

1 Finely chop the fresh parsley and coriander.

2 Beat the garlic, herbs, cumin and butter together with a wooden spoon.

3 Stir in the breadcrumbs and freshly ground black pepper.

4 Spoon a little of the mixture on to each mussel and grill for 2 minutes. Serve garnished with chopped, fresh parsley.

Welsh Rarebit with Anchovies

A classic snack or starter adapted to include salty anchovies. Make as required because the sauce will not keep for long.

INGREDIENTS

Serves 4

40g/1½oz canned anchovies, drained
175g/6oz butter
6 slices of bread, crusts removed
4 large egg yolks
300ml/½ pint/1¼ cups double cream
pinch of cayenne pepper
salt and freshly ground black pepper
15ml/1 tbsp chopped fresh parsley,
    to garnish

1 In a food processor fitted with a metal blade, process the anchovy fillets with two-thirds of the butter. Toast the bread, spread with the anchovy butter, set aside and keep warm.

COOK'S TIP

If you find canned anchovies too salty, soak them briefly in cold water before processing them with the butter.

2 Melt the remaining butter in a small, heavy-based saucepan and beat in the egg yolks.

3 Take off the heat and add the cream. Season to taste, then replace on a low heat. Stir continuously until the sauce is thick. Pour over the toast and sprinkle with the cayenne pepper. Garnish with the chopped fresh parsley.

SALADS

Spinach Salad with Bacon and Prawns

Serve this hot salad with plenty of
crusty bread for mopping up the
delicious juices.

INGREDIENTS

Serves 4

105ml/7 tbsp olive oil

30ml/2 tbsp sherry vinegar

2 garlic cloves, finely chopped

5ml/1 tsp Dijon mustard

12 cooked king prawns

115g/4oz streaky bacon, rinded and cut
  into strips

about 115g/4oz fresh young
  spinach leaves

½ head oak leaf lettuce, roughly torn

salt and freshly ground black pepper

1 To make the dressing, whisk
together 90ml/6 tbsp of the
olive oil with the vinegar, garlic,
mustard and seasoning in a small
pan. Heat gently until thickened
slightly, then keep warm.

2 Carefully peel the prawns,
leaving the tails intact. Set aside.

3 Heat the remaining oil in a
frying pan and fry the bacon
until golden and crisp, stirring
occasionally. Add the prawns and
stir-fry for a few minutes until
warmed through.

4 While the bacon and prawns are
cooking, arrange the spinach
and torn oak leaf lettuce leaves on
four individual serving plates.

5 Spoon the bacon and prawns
on to the leaves, then pour over
the hot dressing. Serve at once.

COOK'S TIP

Sherry vinegar lends its pungent
flavour to this delicious salad.
You can buy it from most large
supermarkets and delicatessens.

Prawn and Artichoke Salad

Artichokes are very popular in Louisiana, where this recipe comes from – and the local cooks are quite willing to use canned hearts.

INGREDIENTS

Serves 4

1 garlic clove

10ml/2 tsp Dijon mustard

60ml/4 tbsp red wine vinegar

150ml/¼ pint/⅔ cup olive oil

45ml/3 tbsp shredded fresh basil leaves or 30ml/2 tbsp finely chopped fresh parsley

1 red onion, very finely sliced

350g/12oz cooked peeled prawns

400g/14oz can artichoke hearts

½ head iceberg lettuce

salt and freshly ground black pepper

1 Coarsely chop the garlic, then crush it to a pulp with 5ml/ 1 tsp salt, using the flat of a heavy knife blade.

2 Mix the garlic and mustard to a paste, then beat in the vinegar and finally the olive oil, beating hard to make a thick creamy dressing. Season with freshly ground black pepper and, if necessary, additional salt.

3 Stir the fresh basil or parsley into the dressing, followed by the sliced onion. Leave to stand for 30 minutes at room temperature, then stir in the prawns and chill in the refrigerator for 1 hour or until ready to serve.

4 Drain the artichoke hearts and halve each one. Shred the lettuce finely.

5 Make a bed of lettuce on a serving platter or 4 individual salad plates and spread the artichoke hearts over it.

6 Immediately before serving, pour the prawns and onion and their marinade over the top of the salad.

Grilled Salmon and Spring Vegetable Salad

Spring is the time to enjoy sweet young vegetables. Cook them briefly, cool to room temperature, dress and serve with a piece of lightly grilled salmon topped with sorrel and quails' eggs.

Serves 4

350g/12oz small new potatoes, scrubbed
    or scraped
4 quails' eggs
115g/4oz young carrots, peeled
115g/4oz baby sweetcorn
115g/4oz sugar snap peas, topped
    and tailed
115g/4oz fine green beans, topped
    and tailed
115g/4oz young courgettes
115g/4oz patty pan squash (optional)
120ml/4fl oz/½ cup French dressing
4 salmon fillets, each weighing 150g/
    5oz, skinned
115g/4oz sorrel or young spinach,
    stems removed
salt and freshly ground black pepper

1 Bring the potatoes to the boil in salted water and cook for 15–20 minutes. Drain, cover and keep warm.

2 Cover the quails' eggs with boiling water and cook for 8 minutes. Refresh under cold water, shell and cut in half.

3 Bring a saucepan of salted water to the boil, add all the other vegetables, except the sorrel or spinach, and cook for about 3 minutes. Drain well. Place the hot vegetables and potatoes in a salad bowl, moisten with a little French dressing and allow to cool.

4 Brush the salmon fillets with French dressing and grill for 6 minutes, turning once.

5 Place the sorrel or spinach in a stainless steel or enamel saucepan with 60ml/4 tbsp French dressing, cover and soften over a gentle heat for 2 minutes. Strain and cool to room temperature. Moisten the vegetables with the remaining dressing.

6 Divide the potatoes and vegetables between 4 large plates, then position a piece of salmon to one side of each plate. Finally, place a spoonful of sorrel or spinach on each piece of salmon and top with 2 halves of a quail's egg. Season to taste and serve at room temperature.

COOK'S TIP

For French dressing, mix together 90ml/6 tbsp olive oil, 30ml/2 tbsp white wine vinegar, 5ml/1 tsp Dijon mustard, 5ml/ 1 tsp sugar, 1 crushed garlic clove and seasoning to taste.

Warm Salmon Salad

Light and fresh, this salad is perfect for an al fresco summer lunch. Serve it immediately, or you'll find the salad leaves will lose their bright colour and texture.

INGREDIENTS

Serves 4

450g/1lb salmon fillet, skinned
30ml/2 tbsp sesame oil
grated rind of ½ orange
juice of 1 orange
5ml/1 tsp Dijon mustard
15ml/1 tbsp chopped fresh tarragon
45ml/3 tbsp groundnut oil
115g/4oz fine green beans, trimmed
175g/6oz mixed salad leaves, such as
    young spinach leaves, radicchio, frisée
    and oak leaf lettuce leaves
15ml/1 tbsp toasted sesame seeds
salt and freshly ground black pepper

1 Cut the salmon into bite-sized pieces, then make the dressing. Mix together the sesame oil, orange rind and juice, mustard, chopped tarragon and seasoning in a bowl. Set aside.

2 Heat the groundnut oil in a frying pan. Add the salmon pieces and fry for 3–4 minutes, until lightly browned but still tender inside.

3 Meanwhile, blanch the green beans in boiling salted water for about 5–6 minutes, until they are tender, but still crisp.

4 Add the dressing to the salmon, toss together gently and cook for 30 seconds. Remove the pan from the heat.

5 Arrange the salad leaves on 4 serving plates. Drain the beans and toss over the leaves. Spoon over the salmon and cooking juices and serve immediately, sprinkled with the sesame seeds.

Salmon and Tuna Parcels

You will need fairly large smoked salmon slices as they are wrapped around a light tuna mixture before being served on a vibrant salad. Kiwi fruit is a particularly rich source of vitamin C.

INGREDIENTS

Serves 4

30ml/2 tbsp low-fat natural yogurt
15ml/1 tbsp sun-dried tomato paste
5ml/1 tsp whole grain honey mustard
grated rind and juice of 1 lime
200g/7oz can tuna in brine, drained
130g/4½oz smoked salmon slices
salt and freshly ground black pepper
fresh mint leaves, to garnish

For the salad

3 tomatoes, sliced
2 kiwi fruit, peeled and sliced
¼ cucumber, cut into julienne sticks

For the mint vinaigrette

15ml/1 tbsp wine vinegar
45ml/3 tbsp olive oil
15ml/1 tbsp chopped fresh mint

COOK'S TIP

Although healthy eating guidelines recommend reducing the amount of fat, particularly saturated fat, in the diet, salad dressings made with polyunsaturated or monounsaturated oil, such as olive oil, can and should be included, in sensible moderation. This recipe is not high in calories, but if weight control is a real issue, use an oil-free dressing instead of vinaigrette.

1 Mix the yogurt, tomato paste and mustard in a bowl. Stir in the grated lime rind and juice. Add the tuna, with black pepper to taste, and mix well.

2 Spread out the salmon slices on a board and spoon some of the tuna mixture on to each piece.

3 Roll up or fold the smoked salmon into neat parcels. Carefully press the edges together to seal.

4 Make the salad. Arrange the tomato and kiwi slices on 4 serving plates. Scatter over the cucumber sticks.

5 Make the vinaigrette. Put all the ingredients in a screw-top jar, season with salt and pepper and shake vigorously. Spoon a little vinaigrette over each salad.

6 Arrange 3–4 salmon parcels on each salad, garnish with the mint leaves and serve.

Avocado and Smoked Fish Salad

Avocado and smoked fish make an excellent combination, and flavoured with herbs and spices, create a delectable salad.

INGREDIENTS

Serves 4

15g/½oz butter or margarine
½ onion, finely sliced
5ml/1 tsp mustard seeds
225g/8oz smoked mackerel, flaked
30ml/2 tbsp chopped, fresh coriander
2 firm tomatoes, skinned and chopped
15ml/1 tbsp lemon juice
salt and freshly ground black pepper

For the salad

2 avocado pears
½ cucumber
15ml/1 tbsp lemon juice
2 firm tomatoes
1 green chilli

1 Melt the butter or margarine in a frying pan, add the onion and mustard seeds and fry for about 5 minutes, until the onion is soft, but not coloured.

2 Add the fish, coriander leaves, tomatoes and lemon juice and cook over a low heat for 2–3 minutes. Remove from the heat and set aside to cool.

3 Make the salad. Peel and thinly slice the avocado pears and slice the cucumber. Put into a bowl and sprinkle with the lemon juice.

4 Slice the tomatoes. Seed and finely chop the chilli.

5 Place the fish mixture in the centre of a serving plate.

6 Arrange the avocado pears, cucumber and tomatoes around the fish. Alternatively, spoon a quarter of the fish mixture on to each of 4 serving plates and divide the avocados, cucumber and tomatoes equally. Sprinkle with the chopped chilli and a little salt and pepper and serve.

Warm Fish Salad with Mango Dressing

This salad is best served during the summer months, preferably out of doors. The dressing combines the flavour of rich mango with hot chilli, ginger and lime.

Serves 4

1 French loaf
4 redfish, black bream or porgy, each
 weighing about 275g/10oz
15ml/1 tbsp vegetable oil
1 mango
1cm/½in fresh root ginger
1 fresh red chilli, seeded and finely
 chopped
30ml/2 tbsp lime juice
30ml/2 tbsp chopped fresh coriander
175g/6oz young spinach
150g/5oz pak choi
175g/6oz cherry tomatoes, halved

1 Cut the French loaf into 20cm/8in lengths. Slice lengthways, then cut into thick fingers. Place the bread on a baking sheet and dry in a preheated oven at 180°C/350°F/Gas 4 for 15 minutes. Slash the fish deeply on both sides with a sharp knife and moisten with oil. Cook under a preheated grill or on a barbecue for 6 minutes, turning once.

2 Peel and stone the mango. Slice the flesh and place half of it in a food processor. Peel and finely grate the ginger, then add to the food processor with the chilli, lime juice and coriander. Process until smooth. Adjust to a pouring consistency with 30–45ml/ 2–3 tbsp water.

3 Wash the salad leaves and spin dry, then divide them equally between 4 serving plates. Place the fish on the leaves. Spoon over the mango dressing and finish with slices of mango and cherry tomato halves. Serve with fingers of crispy French bread.

COOK'S TIP
Other fish suitable for this salad include salmon, monkfish, tuna, sea bass and halibut. Use fillets, cutlets or steaks.

Mediterranean Salad with Basil

A type of Salade Niçoise with pasta, this conjures up all the sunny flavours of the Mediterranean.

INGREDIENTS

Serves 4

225g/8oz chunky pasta shapes
175g/6oz fine green beans
2 large ripe tomatoes
50g/2oz fresh basil leaves
200g/7oz can tuna fish in oil, drained and roughly flaked
2 hard-boiled eggs, shelled and sliced or quartered
50g/2oz can anchovy fillets, drained
salt and freshly ground black pepper
capers and black olives, to garnish

For the dressing
90ml/6 tbsp extra virgin olive oil
30ml/2 tbsp white wine vinegar or lemon juice
2 garlic cloves, crushed
2.5ml/½ tsp Dijon mustard
30ml/2 tbsp chopped fresh basil

1 Whisk all the ingredients for the dressing together, season with salt and pepper and leave to infuse while you make the salad.

2 Cook the pasta in plenty of boiling, salted water according to the manufacturer's instructions. Drain well and set aside to cool.

3 Trim the green beans and blanch them in boiling salted water for 3 minutes. Drain, then refresh in cold water.

4 Slice or quarter the tomatoes and arrange on the base of a bowl. Moisten with a little dressing and cover with a quarter of the basil leaves. Then cover with the beans. Moisten with a little more dressing and cover with a third of the remaining basil.

5 Cover with the pasta tossed in a little more dressing, half the remaining basil and the roughly flaked tuna.

6 Arrange the eggs on top. Finally, scatter over the anchovy fillets, capers and black olives. Pour over the remaining dressing and garnish with the remaining basil. Serve at once. Do not be tempted to chill this salad – all the flavour will be dulled.

COOK'S TIP

Olives marinated in oil flavoured with garlic, herbs and lemon peel would add an extra-special touch to this salad. Choose plump, black olives that are fully ripened. Marinated olives are available from large supermarkets and delicatessens or you could prepare them yourself.

Thai Seafood Salad

This unusual seafood salad with chilli, lemon grass and fish sauce is light and refreshing.

Serves 4

225g/8oz ready-prepared squid
225g/8oz raw tiger prawns
8 scallops, shelled
225g/8oz firm white fish
30–45ml/2–3 tbsp olive oil
small mixed lettuce leaves and coriander
    sprigs, to serve

For the dressing

2 small fresh red chillies, seeded and
    finely chopped
5cm/2in piece lemon grass, finely chopped
2 fresh kaffir lime leaves, shredded
30ml/2 tbsp Thai fish sauce (*nam pla*)
2 shallots, thinly sliced
30ml/2 tbsp lime juice
30ml/2 tbsp rice vinegar
10ml/2 tsp caster sugar

1 Prepare the seafood. Slit open the squid bodies, cut into square pieces, then score the flesh in a criss-cross pattern with a sharp knife. Halve the tentacles, if necessary. Peel and devein the prawns. Remove the dark beard-like fringe and tough muscle from the scallops. Cube the white fish.

2 Heat a wok or large frying pan until hot. Add the oil and swirl it around, then add the prawns and stir-fry for 2–3 minutes until pink. Transfer to a large bowl. Stir-fry the squid and scallops for 1–2 minutes until opaque. Remove and add to the prawns. Stir-fry the white fish for 2–3 minutes. Remove and add to the cooked seafood. Reserve any juices.

3 Put all the dressing ingredients in a small bowl with the reserved juices from the wok or frying pan and mix well.

4 Pour the dressing over the seafood and toss gently. Arrange the salad leaves and coriander sprigs on 4 individual plates, then spoon the seafood on top. Serve at once.

Gado Gado

Gado Gado is a traditional Indonesian salad around which friends and family gather to eat. Fillings are chosen and wrapped in a lettuce leaf. The parcel is then dipped in a spicy peanut sauce and eaten, usually with the left hand. Salad ingredients vary according to what is in season.

INGREDIENTS

Serves 4

2 medium potatoes, peeled

3 eggs

175g/6oz green beans, topped and tailed

1 Cos lettuce

4 tomatoes, cut into wedges

115g/4oz beansprouts

½ cucumber, peeled and cut into fingers

150g/5oz giant white radish, peeled
    and grated

175g/6oz tofu, cut into large dice

350g/12oz large, cooked peeled prawns

1 small bunch fresh coriander

salt

For the spicy peanut sauce

150g/5oz smooth peanut butter

juice of ½ lemon

2 shallots or 1 small onion,
    finely chopped

1 garlic clove, crushed

1–2 small fresh red chillies, seeded and
    finely chopped

30ml/2 tbsp fish sauce (optional)

150ml/¼ pint/⅔ cup coconut milk,
    canned or fresh

15ml/1 tbsp caster sugar

1 To make the peanut sauce, combine the ingredients in a food processor until smooth.

2 Bring the potatoes to the boil in salted water and simmer for 20 minutes. Bring a second pan of salted water to the boil. To save using too many pans, cook the eggs and beans in the same pan.

3 Lower the eggs into the boiling water in the second pan; then, after 6 minutes, add the beans in a steamer for a further 6 minutes. (Hard-boiled eggs should have a total of 12 minutes.) Cool the potatoes, eggs and green beans under cold running water.

4 Wash and spin the salad leaves and use the outer leaves to line a large platter. Pile the remainder to one side of the platter.

5 Slice the potatoes. Shell and quarter the eggs. Arrange the potatoes, eggs, beans and tomatoes in separate piles. Arrange the other salad ingredients and the prawns in a similar way to cover the platter. Garnish with the coriander.

6 Turn the spicy peanut sauce into an attractive bowl and bring to the table with the salad.

HANDLING CHILLIES

Red chillies are considered to be sweeter and hotter than green ones. Smaller varieties of both red and green are likely to be more pungent than larger varieties. You can lessen the intensity of a fresh chilli by splitting it open and removing the white seed-bearing membrane. The residue given off when chillies are cut can cause serious irritation to the skin. Be sure to wash your hands thoroughly after handling raw chillies and avoid touching your eyes or any sensitive skin areas.

Seafood Salad with Fragrant Herbs

This tasty medley of seafood and noodles is a meal in itself.

Serves 4–6

250ml/8fl oz/1 cup fish stock or water
350g/12oz squid, cleaned and cut into rings
12 raw king prawns, peeled and deveined
12 scallops, cleaned
50g/2oz bean thread noodles, soaked in
    warm water for 30 minutes
½ cucumber, cut into thin sticks
1 stalk lemon grass, finely chopped
2 kaffir lime leaves, finely shredded
2 shallots, finely sliced
juice of 1–2 limes
30ml/2 tbsp fish sauce
30ml/2 tbsp chopped spring onion
30ml/2 tbsp coriander leaves
12–15 mint leaves, roughly torn
4 red chillies, seeded and sliced
coriander sprigs, to garnish

1 Pour the fish stock or water into a medium-size saucepan, set over a high heat and bring to the boil.

2 Place each type of seafood individually in the stock and cook for a few minutes. Remove and set aside.

3 Drain the bean thread noodles and cut them into short lengths, about 5cm/2in long. Combine the noodles with the cooked seafood.

4 Add the cucumber, lemon grass, kaffir lime leaves, shallots, lime juice, fish sauce, spring onion, coriander and mint leaves and chillies and mix together well. Serve garnished with the coriander sprigs.

Pomelo Salad

Pomelo is a large, pear-shaped fruit that resembles a grapefruit.

Serves 4-6

30ml/2 tbsp vegetable oil
4 shallots, finely sliced
2 garlic cloves, finely sliced
1 large pomelo
15ml/1 tbsp roasted peanuts
115g/4oz cooked peeled prawns
115g/4oz cooked crab meat
10–12 small mint leaves
2 spring onions, finely sliced
2 red chillies, seeded and finely sliced
coriander leaves, to garnish
shredded fresh coconut (optional)

For the dressing
30ml/2 tbsp fish sauce
15ml/1 tbsp palm or brown sugar
30ml/2 tbsp lime juice

1 Make the dressing. Whisk together the fish sauce, palm or brown sugar and lime juice and set aside.

2 Heat the oil in a small frying pan, add the shallots and garlic and fry for 3–4 minutes, until they are golden. Remove from the pan and set aside.

3 Peel the pomelo and break the flesh into small pieces, taking care to remove any membranes.

4 Coarsely grind the peanuts, then combine with the pomelo flesh, prawns, crab meat, mint leaves and the fried shallot mixture. Toss the salad in the dressing and serve sprinkled with the spring onions, red chillies, coriander leaves and shredded coconut, if using.

Russian Salad

Russian salad became fashionable in the hotel dining rooms of the 1920s and 1930s. Originally it consisted of lightly cooked vegetables, eggs, shellfish and mayonnaise. Today we find it diced in plastic pots in supermarkets. This version recalls better days and plays on the theme of the Fabergé egg.

INGREDIENTS

Serves 4

115g/4oz large button mushrooms
350g/12oz cooked peeled prawns
120ml/4fl oz/½ cup mayonnaise
15ml/1 tbsp lemon juice
1 large gherkin, chopped, or 30ml/
  2 tbsp capers
115g/4oz broad beans, shelled
115g/4oz small new potatoes, scrubbed
  or scraped
115g/4oz young carrots, trimmed
  and peeled
115g/4oz baby sweetcorn
115g/4oz baby turnips, trimmed
15ml/1 tbsp olive oil, preferably French
  or Italian
4 eggs, hard-boiled and shelled
25g/1oz canned anchovy fillets, cut into
  fine strips
salt and freshly ground black pepper
paprika, to garnish

2 Bring a large saucepan of salted water to the boil, add the broad beans and cook for 3 minutes. Drain and cool under cold running water, then pinch the beans between thumb and forefinger to release them from their tough skins. Boil the potatoes for 20 minutes and the remaining vegetables for 6 minutes. Drain and cool under running water.

3 Moisten the vegetables with olive oil and divide between 4 shallow bowls. Spoon on the dressed prawns and place a hard-boiled egg in the centre. Decorate the egg with strips of anchovy and sprinkle with paprika. Serve the remaining mayonnaise separately.

1 Slice the mushrooms, then cut into matchsticks. Mix with the prawns. Combine the mayonnaise and lemon juice and fold half into the mushrooms and prawns, add the gherkin or capers and season.

Melon and Crab Salad

A perfect summer salad when crab and melon are in generous supply.

Serves 6

450g/1lb fresh cooked crab meat
120ml/4fl oz/½ cup mayonnaise
45ml/3 tbsp soured cream or
    natural yogurt
30ml/2 tbsp olive oil
30ml/2 tbsp fresh lemon or lime juice
2–3 spring onions, finely chopped
30ml/2 tbsp finely chopped
    fresh coriander
1.5ml/¼ tsp cayenne pepper
1½ canteloupe or small honeydew melons
3 medium chicory heads
salt and freshly ground black pepper
fresh coriander sprigs, to garnish

1 Pick over the crab meat very carefully, removing any bits of shell or cartilage. Leave the pieces of crab meat as large as possible.

2 In a medium-sized bowl, combine mayonnaise, soured cream or yogurt, olive oil, lemon or lime juice, spring onions, chopped coriander and cayenne pepper and season to taste with salt and pepper. Mix well, then fold the crab meat into this dressing.

3 Halve the melons and remove and discard the seeds. Cut the melons into thin slices, then remove the rind.

4 Divide the salad between 6 individual serving plates, making a decorative design with the melon slices and whole chicory leaves. Place a mound of dressed crab meat on each plate and garnish the salads with one or two fresh coriander sprigs.

Millionaire's Lobster Salad

When money is no object and you're in a decadent mood, this salad will satisfy your every whim. It is ideally served with a cool Chardonnay, Chablis or Pouilly-Fuissé wine.

INGREDIENTS

Serves 4

1 medium lobster, live or cooked

1 bay leaf

1 sprig thyme

700g/1½lb new potatoes, scrubbed

2 ripe tomatoes

4 oranges

½ curly endive lettuce

175g/6oz lamb's lettuce

60ml/4 tbsp extra virgin olive oil

200g/7oz can young artichokes in
    brine, quartered

salt

1 small bunch tarragon, chervil or flat
    leaf parsley, to garnish

For the dressing

30ml/2 tbsp frozen concentrated orange
    juice, thawed

75g/3oz unsalted butter, diced

cayenne pepper

1 If the lobster needs cooking, add to a large pan of salted water with the bay leaf and thyme. Bring to the boil and simmer for 15 minutes. Cool under running water. Twist off the legs and claws, and separate the tail piece from the body section. Break the claws open with a hammer and remove the meat intact. Cut the tail piece open from the underside with a pair of kitchen shears. Slice the meat and set aside.

2 Bring the potatoes to the boil in salted water and simmer for 20 minutes. Drain, cover and keep warm. Cover the tomatoes with boiling water and leave for 20 seconds to loosen their skins. Cool under running water and slip off the skins. Halve the tomatoes, discard the seeds, then cut the flesh into large dice.

3 To segment the oranges, remove the peel from the top, bottom and sides with a serrated knife. With a small paring knife, loosen the orange segments by cutting between the flesh and the membranes, holding the fruit over a small bowl.

4 To make the dressing, measure the thawed orange juice into a glass bowl and set it over a saucepan containing 2.5cm/1in of simmering water. Heat the juice for 1 minute, remove from the heat, then whisk in the butter, a little at a time, until the dressing reaches a coating consistency. Season to taste with salt and a pinch of cayenne pepper, cover and keep warm.

5 Wash the salad leaves and spin dry. Dress with olive oil, then divide between 4 large serving plates. Moisten the potatoes, artichokes and orange segments with olive oil and distribute them among the salad leaves. Lay the sliced lobster over the salad, spoon on the warm butter dressing, add the diced tomato and decorate with sprigs of fresh tarragon, chervil or flat leaf parsley. Serve at room temperature.

Smoked Trout Salad

Horseradish is as good a partner to smoked trout as it is to roast beef. In this recipe it combines with yogurt to make a deliciously piquant light salad dressing.

INGREDIENTS

Serves 4

1 oak leaf or other red lettuce

225g/8oz small tomatoes, cut into
    thin wedges

½ cucumber, peeled and thinly sliced

4 smoked trout fillets, about 200g/7oz
    each, skinned and flaked

For the dressing

pinch of English mustard powder

15–20ml/3–4 tsp white wine vinegar

30ml/2 tbsp light olive oil

100ml/3½fl oz/scant ½ cup natural yogurt

about 30ml/2 tbsp grated fresh or
    bottled horseradish

pinch of caster sugar

1 First, make the dressing. Mix together the mustard powder and vinegar, then gradually whisk in the oil, yogurt, horseradish and sugar. Set aside for 30 minutes.

> ## COOK'S TIP
> ～
> Salt should not be necessary in this recipe because of the saltiness of the smoked trout.

2 Place the lettuce leaves in a large bowl. Stir the dressing again, then pour half of it over the leaves and toss them lightly using two spoons.

3 Arrange the lettuce on 4 individual plates with the tomatoes, cucumber and trout. Spoon over the remaining dressing and serve at once.

Tuna and Bean Salad

This substantial salad makes a good light meal and can be assembled from canned ingredients quickly.

INGREDIENTS

Serves 4–6

2 x 400g/14oz cans cannellini or
   borlotti beans
2 x 200g/7oz cans tuna fish, drained
60ml/4 tbsp extra virgin olive oil
30ml/2 tbsp fresh lemon juice
15ml/1 tbsp chopped fresh parsley
3 spring onions, thinly sliced
salt and freshly ground black pepper

1 Pour the beans into a large strainer and rinse under cold water. Drain well. Place in a serving dish.

2 Break the tuna into fairly large flakes and arrange over the beans in the serving dish.

3 In a small bowl make the dressing by combining the oil with the lemon juice. Season with salt and pepper and stir in the parsley. Mix well. Pour over the beans and tuna.

4 Sprinkle with the spring onions. Toss the salad well before serving.

Provençal Salad

*There are probably as many versions
of this salad as there are cooks in
Provence. With chunks of good
French bread, this regional classic
makes a wonderful summer lunch
or light supper.*

Serves 4–6

225g/8oz French beans
450g/1lb new potatoes, peeled and cut
　　into 2.5cm/1 in pieces
white wine vinegar and olive oil,
　　for sprinkling
1 small Cos or round lettuce, washed,
　　dried and torn into bite-sized pieces
4 ripe plum tomatoes, quartered
1 small cucumber, peeled, seeded
　　and diced
1 green or red pepper, thinly sliced
4 hard-boiled eggs, shelled and quartered
24 Niçoise or black olives
225g/8oz can tuna in brine, drained
50g/2oz can anchovy fillets in olive
　　oil, drained
basil leaves, to garnish
garlic croûtons, to serve

For the anchovy vinaigrette
20ml/4 tsp Dijon mustard
50g/2oz can anchovy fillets in olive
　　oil, drained
1 garlic clove, crushed
60ml/4 tbsp lemon juice or white
　　wine vinegar
120ml/4fl oz/½ cup sunflower oil
120ml/4fl oz/½ cup extra virgin olive oil
freshly ground black pepper

1 First, make the anchovy
vinaigrette. Place the mustard,
anchovies and garlic in a bowl and
blend together by pressing the
garlic and anchovies against the
sides of the bowl. Season well with
pepper. Using a small whisk, blend
in the lemon juice or wine vinegar.
Slowly whisk in the sunflower oil
in a thin stream and then the olive
oil, whisking until the dressing is
smooth and creamy.

2 Alternatively, put all the
dressing ingredients except the
oil in a food processor fitted with
the metal blade and process. With
the machine running, slowly add
the oils, in a thin stream, until the
vinaigrette is thick and creamy.

4 Add the potatoes to the same
boiling water, reduce the heat
and simmer for 10–15 minutes,
until just tender, then drain.
Sprinkle with a little vinegar and
olive oil and a spoonful of the
anchovy vinaigrette.

5 Arrange the lettuce on a
platter, top with the tomatoes,
cucumber and pepper, then add
the French beans and potatoes.

6 Arrange the eggs, olives, tuna
and anchovies on top and
garnish with the basil leaves.
Drizzle over the remaining
anchovy vinaigrette and serve with
garlic croûtons.

3 Drop the French beans into a
large saucepan of boiling water
and boil for 3 minutes until tender,
yet crisp. Transfer the beans to a
colander with a slotted spoon, then
rinse under cold running water.
Drain again and set aside.

COOK'S TIP

To make garlic croûtons, thinly
slice a French stick or cut larger
loaves into 2.5cm/1in cubes.
Place the bread in a single layer
on a baking sheet and bake in a
preheated 180°C/350°F/Gas 4
oven for 7–10 minutes or until
golden, turning once. Rub the
toast with a garlic clove and
serve hot or allow to cool, then
store in an airtight container to
serve at room temperature.

Prawn Salad with Curry Dressing

Curry spices add an unexpected twist to this salad. Warm flavours combine especially well with sweet prawns and grated apple.

INGREDIENTS

Serves 4

1 ripe tomato
½ iceberg lettuce, shredded
1 small onion
1 small bunch fresh coriander
15ml/1 tbsp lemon juice
450g/1lb cooked peeled prawns
1 apple, peeled
salt
8 whole cooked prawns, 8 lemon wedges
   and 4 sprigs fresh coriander, to garnish

For the dressing

75ml/5 tbsp mayonnaise
5ml/1 tsp mild curry paste
15ml/1 tbsp tomato ketchup
30ml/2 tbsp water

1 To peel the tomato, pierce the skin with a knife and immerse in boiling water for 20 seconds. Drain and cool under running water. Peel off the skin. Halve the tomato, push the seeds out with your thumb and discard them. Cut the flesh into large dice.

2 Finely shred the lettuce, onion and coriander. Add the tomato, moisten with lemon juice and season with salt.

3 To make the dressing, mix together the mayonnaise, curry paste and tomato ketchup in a small bowl. Add the water to thin the dressing and season to taste with salt.

4 Combine the prawns with the dressing. Quarter and core the apple and grate into the mixture.

5 Distribute the shredded lettuce and onion mixture between 4 plates or bowls. Pile the prawn mixture in the centre of each and garnish with 2 whole prawns, 2 lemon wedges and a sprig of coriander.

COOK'S TIP

Fresh coriander is inclined to wilt if it is not kept in water. Store it in a jar of water, covered with a plastic bag, in the refrigerator and it will stay fresh for several days.

Aubergine Salad with Dried Shrimps

An appetizing and unusual salad that you will find yourself making over and over again.

Serves 4–6

2 aubergines

15ml/1 tbsp oil

30ml/2 tbsp dried shrimps, soaked
    and drained

15ml/1 tbsp coarsely chopped garlic

30ml/2 tbsp freshly squeezed lime juice

5ml/1 tsp palm or brown sugar

30ml/2 tbsp fish sauce

1 hard-boiled egg, shelled and chopped

4 shallots, finely sliced into rings

coriander leaves and 2 red chillies, seeded
    and sliced, to garnish

3 Heat the oil in a small frying
pan, add the drained shrimps
and garlic and fry for 3–4 minutes,
until golden. Remove from the pan
and set aside.

4 To make the dressing, put the
lime juice, palm or brown
sugar and fish sauce in a small
bowl and whisk together.

5 To serve, arrange the
aubergines on a serving dish.
Top with the egg, shallots and
dried shrimp mixture. Drizzle over
the dressing and garnish with
coriander and chillies.

COOK'S TIP

For an interesting variation, try
using salted ducks' or quails'
eggs, cut in half, instead of
chopped hens' eggs.

1 Grill or roast the aubergines
until charred and tender.

2 When the aubergines are cool
enough to handle, peel away
the skin and slice the flesh.

Thai Dipping Sauce

This is a delicious and traditional accompaniment to Hot Coconut Prawn and Pawpaw Salad.

INGREDIENTS

Makes 120ml/4fl oz/½ cup

15ml/1 tbsp vegetable oil

1cm/½in square shrimp paste, or 15ml/
1 tbsp fish sauce

2 garlic cloves, finely sliced

2cm/¾in piece fresh root ginger, peeled
and finely chopped

3 small red chillies, seeded and chopped

15ml/1 tbsp finely chopped coriander root
or stem

20ml/4 tsp sugar

45ml/3 tbsp dark soy sauce

juice of ½ lime

1 Heat the vegetable oil in a wok, add the shrimp paste or fish sauce, garlic, ginger and chillies and soften without colouring, for about 1–2 minutes.

2 Remove from the heat and add the coriander, sugar, soy sauce and lime juice. The sauce will keep in a screw-top jar for up to 10 days.

Hot Coconut Prawn and Pawpaw Salad

This exotic salad may be served with many oriental beef and chicken dishes.

INGREDIENTS

Serves 4-6

225g/8oz raw or cooked prawn tails,
peeled and deveined

2 ripe pawpaws

225g/8oz mixed lettuce leaves, Chinese
leaves and young spinach

1 firm tomato, skinned, seeded and
roughly chopped

3 spring onions, shredded

1 small bunch coriander, shredded,
1 large chilli, sliced, and 1 turnip,
carved, to garnish

Thai Dipping Sauce, to serve

For the dressing

15ml/1 tbsp creamed coconut

30ml/2 tbsp boiling water

90ml/6 tbsp vegetable oil

juice of 1 lime

2.5ml/½ tsp hot chilli sauce

10ml/2 tsp fish sauce (optional)

5ml/1 tsp sugar

1 To make the dressing, place the creamed coconut in a screw-top jar and add the boiling water to soften. Add the vegetable oil, lime juice, chilli sauce, fish sauce, if using, and sugar. Shake well and set aside. Do not refrigerate.

2 If using raw prawn tails, cover with cold water in a saucepan, bring to the boil and simmer for no longer than 2 minutes. Drain and set aside.

3 To prepare the pawpaws, cut each in half from top to bottom and remove the black seeds with a teaspoon. Peel away the outer skin and cut the flesh into even-sized pieces. Wash the salad leaves and toss in a bowl. Add the other ingredients. Pour on the dressing, garnish with the coriander, chilli and turnip, and serve with Thai Dipping Sauce.

PASTA AND
RICE

Pasta with Tuna, Capers and Anchovies

This piquant sauce could be made without the addition of tomatoes – just heat the oil, add the other ingredients and heat through gently before tossing with the pasta.

INGREDIENTS

Serves 4

400g/14oz canned tuna fish in oil
30ml/2 tbsp olive oil
2 garlic cloves, crushed
800g/1¾lb canned chopped tomatoes
6 canned anchovy fillets, drained
30ml/2 tbsp capers in vinegar, drained
30ml/2 tbsp chopped fresh basil
450g/1lb/4 cups rigatoni, penne
   or garganelle
salt and freshly ground black pepper
fresh basil sprigs, to garnish

1 Drain the oil from the tuna into a heavy-based saucepan, add the olive oil and heat gently until it stops 'spitting'.

2 Add the garlic and fry until golden. Stir in the tomatoes, lower the heat and simmer for 25 minutes until thickened.

3 Flake the tuna and cut the anchovies in half. Stir into the sauce with the capers and chopped basil. Season well.

4 Cook the pasta in plenty of boiling salted water according to the manufacturer's instructions. Drain well and toss with the sauce. Garnish with fresh basil sprigs.

Farfalle with Smoked Salmon and Dill

This quick, luxurious and quite delicious sauce for pasta has now become very fashionable in Italy.

INGREDIENTS

Serves 4

6 spring onions, sliced

50g/2oz butter

90ml/6 tbsp dry white wine or vermouth

450ml/¾ pint/1⅞ cups double cream

freshly grated nutmeg

225g/8oz smoked salmon

30ml/2 tbsp chopped fresh dill

freshly squeezed lemon juice

450g/1lb farfalle (pasta bows)

salt and freshly ground black pepper

fresh dill sprigs, to garnish

1 Slice the spring onions finely. Melt the butter in a saucepan and fry the spring onions for about 1 minute, until softened.

2 Add the wine and boil hard to reduce to about 30ml/2 tbsp. Stir in the cream and add salt, pepper and nutmeg to taste. Bring to the boil and simmer for 2–3 minutes until slightly thickened.

3 Cut the smoked salmon into 2.5cm/1in squares and stir into the sauce, together with the dill. Add a little lemon juice to taste. Keep warm.

4 Cook the pasta in plenty of boiling salted water as directed. Drain well. Toss with the sauce and serve immediately, garnished with sprigs of dill.

Tagliatelle with Smoked Salmon

This is a pretty pasta sauce that tastes as good as it looks. The light texture of the cucumber perfectly complements the fish. Different effects and colour combinations can be achieved by using green, white or red tagliatelle – or even a mixture of all three.

INGREDIENTS

Serves 4

350g/12oz dried or fresh tagliatelle
½ cucumber
75g/3oz butter
grated rind of 1 orange
30ml/2 tbsp chopped fresh dill
300ml/½ pint/1¼ cups single cream
15ml/1 tbsp orange juice
115g/4oz smoked salmon, skinned
salt and freshly ground black pepper

1 If using dried pasta, cook in lightly salted boiling water following the manufacturer's instructions on the packet. If using fresh pasta, cook in lightly salted boiling water for 2–3 minutes, or until just tender but still firm to the bite.

2 Using a sharp knife, cut the cucumber in half lengthways, then using a small spoon scoop out the cucumber seeds and discard.

3 Turn the cucumber on to the flat side and slice it thinly.

4 Melt the butter in a heavy-based saucepan, add the grated orange rind and fresh dill and stir well. Add the cucumber and cook gently over a low heat for about 2 minutes, stirring from time to time.

5 Add the cream, orange juice and seasoning to taste and simmer gently for 1 minute.

6 Meanwhile, cut the salmon into thin strips.

7 Stir the salmon into the sauce and heat through.

8 Drain the pasta thoroughly and toss it in the sauce. Serve immediately.

COOK'S TIP

A more economical way to make this special-occasion sauce is to use smoked salmon pieces, sold relatively inexpensively by most delicatessens and some super-markets. (These are just off-cuts and awkwardly shaped pieces that are unsuitable for recipes requiring whole slices of smoked salmon.) Smoked trout is a less expensive alternative, but it lacks the rich flavour and colour of smoked salmon.

Prawn and Pasta Salad with Green Dressing

Anchovies need a nice strong dressing to match their flavour.

INGREDIENTS

Serves 4-6

4 anchovy fillets, drained
60ml/4 tbsp milk
225g/8oz squid
15ml/1 tbsp chopped capers
15ml/1 tbsp chopped gherkins
1–2 garlic cloves, crushed
150ml/¼ pint/⅔ cup natural yogurt
30–45ml/2–3 tbsp mayonnaise
squeeze of lemon juice
50g/2oz watercress, chopped finely
30ml/2 tbsp chopped fresh parsley
30ml/2 tbsp chopped fresh basil
350g/12oz fusilli (pasta spirals)
350g/12oz cooked peeled prawns
salt and freshly ground black pepper

1 Put the anchovies into a small bowl and cover with the milk. Leave to soak for 10 minutes. Pull the heads from the squid and remove and discard the quills. Peel the outer speckled skin from the bodies and rinse well. Cut into 5mm/¼in rings. Cut the tentacles from the heads, rinse under cold water and cut into 5mm/¼in slices.

2 To make the dressing, mix the capers, gherkins, garlic, yogurt, mayonnaise, lemon juice and fresh herbs in a bowl. Drain and chop the anchovies. Add to the dressing with the seasoning.

3 Drop the squid rings and tentacles into a large pan of boiling, salted water. Lower the heat and simmer for 1–2 minutes (do not overcook or the squid will become tough). Remove with a slotted spoon. Cook the pasta in the same water according to the instructions on the packet. Drain thoroughly.

4 Mix the prawns and squid into the dressing in a large bowl. Add the pasta, toss and serve immediately. Alternatively, allow to cool and serve as a salad.

Noodles with Tomatoes and Prawns

*Influences from Italy and the East
combine in a dish with a lovely
texture and taste.*

INGREDIENTS

Serves 4

350g/12oz somen noodles

45ml/3 tbsp olive oil

20 raw king prawns, peeled and deveined

2 garlic cloves, finely chopped

45–60ml/3–4 tbsp sun-dried tomato paste

salt and freshly ground black pepper

For the garnish

handful of basil leaves

30ml/2 tbsp sun-dried tomatoes in oil,
    drained and cut into strips

1 Cook the noodles in a large
saucepan of boiling water until
tender, following the directions on
the packet. Drain well.

2 Heat half the oil in a large
frying pan. Add the prawns
and garlic and fry them over a
medium heat for 3–5 minutes,
until the prawns turn pink and are
firm to the touch.

3 Stir in 15ml/1 tbsp of the sun-
dried tomato paste and mix
well. Using a slotted spoon,
transfer the prawns to a bowl and
keep hot.

4 Reheat the oil remaining in
the pan. Stir in the rest of the
oil with the remaining sun-dried
tomato paste. You may need to add
a spoonful of water if the mixture
is very thick.

5 When the mixture starts to
sizzle, toss in the well-drained
noodles. Add salt and pepper to
taste and mix well.

6 Return the prawns to the pan
and toss to combine. Serve at
once, garnished with the basil and
strips of sun-dried tomatoes.

COOK'S TIP

Ready-made sun-dried tomato
paste is widely available.
However, you can make your
own simply by processing
bottled sun-dried tomatoes with
their oil. You could also add a
couple of anchovy fillets and
some capers if you like.

Linguine with Clams

Toss together this sauce for a real seafood flavour and serve with a light mixed salad. Canned clams make this a speedy sauce for those in a real hurry.

INGREDIENTS

Serves 4

350g/12oz linguine (thin noodles)
25g/1oz butter
2 leeks, thinly sliced
150ml/¼ pint/⅔ cup dry white wine
4 tomatoes, skinned, seeded and chopped
pinch of ground turmeric (optional)
250g/9oz can clams, drained
30ml/2 tbsp chopped fresh basil
60ml/4 tbsp crème fraîche
salt and freshly ground black pepper

1 Cook the pasta following the instructions on the packet.

2 Meanwhile, melt the butter in a small saucepan and fry the leeks for about 5 minutes until softened, but not coloured.

3 Add the wine, tomatoes and turmeric, if using, bring to the boil and boil until reduced by half.

4 Stir in the clams, basil, crème fraîche and seasoning to taste and heat through gently without allowing the sauce to boil.

5 Drain the pasta thoroughly and toss it in the sauce to coat. Serve immediately.

Macaroni with King Prawns and Ham

This quick-and-easy recipe is an ideal lunch or supper dish.

INGREDIENTS

Serves 4

350g/12oz short macaroni
45ml/3 tbsp olive oil
12 raw king prawns, peeled and deveined
1 garlic clove, chopped
175g/6oz smoked ham, diced
150ml/¼ pint/⅔ cup red wine
½ small radicchio lettuce, shredded
2 egg yolks, beaten
30ml/2 tbsp chopped fresh flat leaf parsley
150ml/¼ pint/⅔ cup double cream
salt and freshly ground black pepper
shredded fresh basil, to garnish

1 Cook the pasta following the instructions on the packet.

2 Meanwhile, heat the oil in a frying pan and cook the prawns, garlic and ham for about 5 minutes, stirring occasionally, until the prawns are tender.

3 Add the wine and radicchio, bring to the boil and boil rapidly until the juices are reduced by about half.

4 Stir in the egg yolks, parsley and cream and bring almost to the boil, stirring constantly, then simmer until the sauce thickens slightly. Season to taste.

5 Drain the pasta thoroughly and toss it in the sauce to coat. Serve immediately, garnished with shredded fresh basil.

COOK'S TIP

Flat leaf parsley has more flavour than the curly variety. Finely chop any leftover parsley and freeze it in a small plastic bag. It is then ready to use for cooking, but not garnishing.

Pasta with Scallops in Green Sauce

The striking colours of this dish make it irresistible.

INGREDIENTS

Serves 4

120ml/4fl oz/½ cup low-fat crème fraîche
10ml/2 tsp wholegrain mustard
2 garlic cloves, crushed
30–45ml/2–3 tbsp fresh lime juice
60ml/4 tbsp chopped fresh parsley
30ml/2 tbsp snipped chives
350g/12oz black tagliatelle
12 large, prepared scallops
60ml/4 tbsp white wine
150ml/¼ pint/⅔ cup fish stock
salt and freshly ground black pepper
lime wedges and parsley sprigs, to garnish

1 To make the green sauce, mix the crème fraîche, mustard, garlic, lime juice, herbs and seasoning together in a bowl.

2 Cook the pasta in boiling, salted water according to the packet instructions. Drain well.

3 Slice the scallops in half, horizontally. Keep any coral whole. Put the wine and fish stock into a saucepan. Heat to simmering point. Add the scallops and cook very gently for 3–4 minutes.

4 Remove the scallops. Boil the wine and stock vigorously to reduce by half and add the green sauce to the pan. Heat gently to warm, replace the scallops and cook for 1 minute. Spoon over the pasta and garnish with lime wedges and parsley.

Pasta with Scallops in Tomato Sauce

Delicate and simple, this pasta dish makes a good starter or main dish.

INGREDIENTS

Serves 4

450g/1lb long, thin pasta, such as fettucine or linguine

30ml/2 tbsp olive oil

2 garlic cloves, finely chopped

450g/1lb prepared scallops, sliced in half horizontally

30ml/2 tbsp chopped fresh basil

salt and freshly ground black pepper

salt

fresh basil sprigs, to garnish

For the sauce

30ml/2 tbsp olive oil

½ onion, finely chopped

1 garlic clove, finely chopped

2 x 400g/14oz cans peeled tomatoes

1 To make the sauce, heat the oil in a non-stick frying pan. Add the onion, garlic and a little salt, and cook for about 5 minutes, stirring occasionally, until just softened, but not coloured.

2 Add the tomatoes, with their juice, and crush with a fork. Bring to the boil, then lower the heat and simmer gently for 15 minutes. Remove the pan from the heat and set aside.

3 Bring a large pan of salted water to the boil. Add the pasta and cook until just tender to the bite, according to the instructions on the packet.

4 Meanwhile, combine the oil and garlic in another non-stick frying pan and cook for about 30 seconds, until just sizzling. Add the scallops and 2.5ml/½ tsp salt and cook over a high heat for about 3 minutes, tossing, until the scallops are cooked through.

5 Add the scallops to the tomato sauce. Season with salt and pepper to taste, then stir gently and keep warm.

6 Drain the pasta, rinse under hot water, and drain. Add the scallop sauce and the basil and toss thoroughly. Serve immediately, garnished with fresh basil sprigs.

Spaghettini with Vodka and Caviar

This is an elegant, yet easy, way to serve spaghettini. In Rome it is an after-theatre favourite.

INGREDIENTS

Serves 4

60ml/4 tbsp olive oil

3 spring onions, thinly sliced

1 garlic clove, finely chopped

120ml/4fl oz/½ cup vodka

150ml/¼ pint/⅔ cup double cream

150ml/¼ pint/⅔ cup black or red caviar

400g/14oz spaghettini

salt and freshly ground black pepper

COOK'S TIP

The finest caviar is salted sturgeon roe. Red 'caviar' is dog salmon roe, cheaper and often saltier than sturgeon roe.

1 Heat the oil in a small frying pan. Add the spring onions and garlic, and cook gently for 4–5 minutes, until softened.

2 Add the vodka and cream, and cook over low heat for about 5–8 minutes more.

3 Remove from the heat and stir in the caviar. Season with salt and pepper, as necessary.

4 Meanwhile, cook the pasta in a large pan of rapidly boiling salted water until tender, but still firm to the bite. Drain the pasta, and toss immediately to coat with the sauce. Serve at once.

Penne with Tuna and Mozzarella

This tasty sauce is quickly made from store-cupboard ingredients, with the simple addition of fresh mozzarella and parsley. If possible, use tuna canned in olive oil.

INGREDIENTS

Serves 4

400g/14oz penne, or other short pasta

15ml/1 tbsp capers, in brine or salt

2 garlic cloves

45g/3 tbsp chopped fresh parsley

200g/7oz can of tuna, drained

75ml/5 tbsp olive oil

salt and freshly ground black pepper

115g/4oz mozzarella cheese, cut into small dice

1 Bring a pan of salted water to the boil and cook the pasta according to packet instructions.

2 Rinse the capers well in water. Chop them finely with the garlic. Combine with the parsley and the tuna. Stir in the oil, and season to taste.

3 Drain the pasta when it is just tender, but still firm to the bite. Tip it into a large frying pan. Add the tuna sauce and the diced mozzarella. Cook over moderate heat, stirring constantly, until the cheese is just beginning to melt. Serve at once.

Black Pasta with Squid Sauce

Tagliatelle flavoured with squid ink looks amazing and tastes deliciously of the sea. You'll find it in good Italian delicatessens.

INGREDIENTS

Serves 4

105ml/7 tbsp olive oil

2 shallots, chopped

2 garlic cloves, crushed

45ml/3 tbsp chopped fresh parsley

675g/1½lb cleaned squid, cut into rings
    and rinsed

150ml/¼ pint/⅔ cup dry white wine

400g/14oz can chopped tomatoes

2.5ml/½ tsp dried chilli flakes or powder

450g/1lb black tagliatelle

salt and fresh ground black pepper

1 Heat the oil in a pan and add the shallots. Cook until pale golden in colour, then add the garlic. When the garlic colours a little, then add 30ml/2 tbsp of the parsley, stir, then add the squid and stir again. Cook for 3–4 minutes, then add the wine.

2 Simmer for a few seconds, then add the tomatoes and chilli flakes or powder and season with salt and pepper to taste. Cover and simmer gently for about 1 hour, until the squid is tender. Add more water if necessary.

3 Cook the pasta in plenty of boiling salted water, according to the instructions on the packet, until tender, but still firm to the bite. Drain and return the pasta to the pan. Add the squid sauce and mix well. Sprinkle each serving with the remaining chopped parsley and serve at once.

COOK'S TIP

The labelling of olive oil can be confusing. The oil is basically divided into two types – pure and virgin. The latter comes from the first pressing, but virgin olive oil is further sub-divided, according to its level of acidity. The least acid and so the best oil is extra virgin. Use this quality for special dishes and salad dressings, but the next best oil – virgin – may be used for general cooking. Pure olive oil, although not in any way adulterated, lacks the unique flavour of virgin oil.

Tagliatelle with Saffron Mussels

Mussels in a saffron and cream sauce are served with tagliatelle in this recipe, but you can use any other pasta, as you prefer.

Serves 4

1.75kg/4–4½lb mussels
150ml/¼ pint/⅔ cup dry white wine
2 shallots, chopped
350g/12oz dried tagliatelle
25g/1oz butter
2 garlic cloves, crushed
250ml/8fl oz/1 cup double cream
generous pinch of saffron strands, soaked
   in 30ml/2 tbsp hot water
1 egg yolk
salt and freshly ground black pepper
30ml/2 tbsp chopped fresh parsley,
   to garnish

1 Scrub the mussels under cold running water. Remove the beards. Discard any mussels with damaged shells or that do not shut immediately when sharply tapped.

2 Place the mussels in a large pan with the wine and shallots. Cover and cook over a high heat, shaking the pan occasionally, for 5–8 minutes, until the mussels have opened. Drain the mussels, reserving the liquid. Discard any that remain closed. Shell all but a few of the mussels and keep warm.

3 Bring the reserved cooking liquid to the boil, then boil vigorously to reduce by about half. Strain through a fine sieve into a jug to remove any grit.

4 Cook the tagliatelle in a pan of boiling salted water, according to the packet instructions, until tender, but still firm to the bite.

5 Melt the butter in a pan and fry the garlic for 1 minute. Add the mussel liquid, cream and saffron. Heat gently until the sauce thickens slightly. Remove from the heat and stir in the egg yolk, shelled mussels and seasoning.

6 Drain the pasta and transfer to serving bowls. Spoon over the sauce and sprinkle with chopped parsley. Garnish with the mussels in shells and serve at once.

Sicilian Spaghetti with Sardines

A traditional dish from Sicily, with ingredients that are common to many parts of the Mediterranean.

INGREDIENTS

Serves 4

12 fresh sardines, cleaned and boned
250ml/8fl oz/1 cup olive oil
1 onion, chopped
25g/1oz fresh dill, chopped
50g/2oz pine nuts
25g/1oz raisins, soaked in water
50g/2oz fresh breadcrumbs
450g/1lb spaghetti
flour for dusting
salt

1 Wash the sardines and pat them dry on kitchen paper. Open them out flat, then cut in half lengthways.

2 Heat 30ml/2 tbsp of the oil in a pan, add the onion and fry until golden. Add the dill and cook gently for 1–2 minutes. Add the pine nuts and raisins and season with salt to taste. Dry-fry the breadcrumbs in a frying pan until golden. Set aside.

3 Cook the spaghetti in boiling, salted water according to the instructions on the packet, until tender, but still firm to the bite. Heat the remaining oil in a pan. Dust the sardines with flour and fry in the hot oil for 2–3 minutes. Drain on kitchen paper.

4 Drain the spaghetti and return to the pan. Add the onion mixture and toss well to coat. Transfer the spaghetti mixture to a warmed serving platter and arrange the fried sardines on top. Sprinkle with the toasted bread-crumbs and serve immediately.

COOK'S TIP
~

Sardines are actually baby pilchards and weigh about 115g/4oz. They are covered in very fine scales and these are most easily removed with your hand, rather than with a scaling knife. Hold the fish by the tail under cold running water and rub your thumb and fingers gently along the body down to the head.

Smoked Haddock and Pasta in Parsley Sauce

A creamy and delicious pasta dish with a crunchy almond topping.

INGREDIENTS

Serves 4

450g/1lb smoked haddock fillet
1 small leek or onion, sliced thickly
300ml/½ pint/1¼ cups milk
1 bouquet garni (bay leaf, thyme and
    parsley stalks)
25g/1oz margarine
25g/1oz plain flour
225g/8oz pasta shells
30ml/2 tbsp chopped fresh parsley
salt and freshly ground black pepper
15g/½oz toasted flaked almonds,
    to garnish

3 Put the margarine, flour and reserved milk into a pan. Bring to the boil and whisk constantly until smooth. Season, then add the fish and leek or onion.

4 Cook the pasta in a large pan of boiling water until tender, but still firm to the bite. Drain and stir into the sauce with the chopped parsley. Serve at once, scattered with almonds.

1 Remove all the skin and any bones from the haddock. Put into a pan with the leek or onion, milk and bouquet garni. Bring to the boil, cover and simmer gently for about 8–10 minutes, until the fish flakes easily.

2 Strain, reserving the milk for making the sauce, and discard the bouquet garni.

Baked Seafood Spaghetti

In this dish, each portion is baked and served in an individual parcel, which is then opened at the table. Use oven parchment or aluminium foil to make the parcels.

INGREDIENTS

Serves 4

450g/1lb fresh mussels
120ml/4fl oz/½ cup dry white wine
60ml/4 tbsp olive oil
2 garlic cloves, finely chopped
450g/1lb tomatoes, fresh or canned,
    peeled and finely chopped
400g/14oz spaghetti or other long pasta
225g/8oz fresh or frozen and thawed,
    uncooked peeled prawns, deveined
30ml/2 tbsp chopped fresh parsley
salt and freshly ground black pepper

1 Scrub the mussels well under cold running water, cutting off the beards with a small sharp knife. Discard any with broken shells or which do not close immediately when sharply tapped. Place the mussels and the wine in a large saucepan and heat until they open.

2 Lift out the mussels and remove to a side dish. Discard any that do not open. Strain the cooking liquid through clean muslin to remove any grit and reserve until needed.

3 In a medium saucepan, heat the oil and garlic together for 1–2 minutes. Add the tomatoes, and cook over moderate to high heat until they soften. Stir in 175ml/6fl oz/¾ cup of the reserved cooking liquid from the mussels and simmer gently.

4 Meanwhile, cook the pasta in a large pan of boiling salted water, according to the packet instructions, until tender, but still firm to the bite.

5 Just before draining the pasta, add the prawns and parsley to the tomato sauce. Simmer for a further 2 minutes, or until the prawns are cooked through. Taste and adjust the seasoning, if necessary. Remove from the heat and set aside. Drain the pasta.

6 Prepare 4 pieces of parchment paper or foil approximately 30cm x 45cm (12in x 18in). Place each sheet in the centre of a shallow bowl. Turn the drained pasta into a mixing bowl. Add the tomato sauce and mix well. Stir in the mussels.

7 Divide the pasta and seafood between the 4 pieces of paper or foil, placing a mound in the centre of each, and twisting the paper ends together to make a closed packet. (The bowl under the paper will stop the sauce from spilling while the paper parcels are being closed.) Arrange on a large baking tray and bake in a preheated oven at 150°C/300°F/ Gas 2 for 8–10 minutes. Place an unopened packet on each of 4 individual serving plates.

Fusilli with Smoked Trout

The smoked trout and creamy sauce blend beautifully with the still crunchy vegetables.

INGREDIENTS

Serves 4–6

2 carrots, cut into julienne sticks

1 leek, cut into julienne sticks

2 sticks celery, cut into julienne sticks

150ml/¼ pint/⅔ cup vegetable stock

225g/8oz smoked trout fillets, skinned
  and cut into strips

200g/7oz cream cheese

150ml/¼ pint/⅔ cup medium sweet white
  wine or fish stock

15ml/1 tbsp chopped fresh dill or fennel

225g/8oz long curly fusilli

salt and freshly ground black pepper

dill sprigs, to garnish

1 Put the carrots, leek and celery into a pan with the vegetable stock. Bring to the boil and cook quickly for 4–5 minutes, until tender and most of the stock has evaporated. Remove from the heat and add the smoked trout.

2 To make the sauce, put the cream cheese and wine or fish stock into a saucepan, heat and whisk until smooth. Season with salt and pepper. Add the chopped dill or fennel.

3 Cook the fusilli in a pan of boiling, salted water according to the packet instructions, until tender, but firm to the bite. Drain thoroughly.

4 Return the fusilli to the pan with the sauce, toss lightly and transfer to a serving bowl. Top with the cooked vegetables and trout. Serve immediately, garnished with dill sprigs.

Spaghetti with Hot-and-sour Fish

A truly Chinese spicy taste is what
makes this sauce so different.

INGREDIENTS

Serves 4

350g/12oz spaghetti tricolore

450g/1lb monkfish, skinned

225g/8oz courgettes

1 fresh green chilli, cored and seeded

15ml/1 tbsp olive oil

1 large onion, chopped

5ml/1 tsp turmeric

115g/4oz shelled peas, thawed if frozen

10ml/2 tsp lemon juice

75ml/5 tbsp hoisin sauce

150ml/¼ pint/⅔ cup water

salt and freshly ground black pepper

dill sprig, to garnish

1 Cook the pasta in boiling salted water according to the instructions on the packet, until tender, but still firm to the bite.

2 Meanwhile, with a sharp knife, cut the monkfish into bite-sized pieces.

COOK'S TIP

This dish is quite low in calories, so it is ideal for slimmers. Hoisin sauce is widely available from most supermarkets or Chinese food stores.

3 Thinly slice the courgettes, then finely chop the fresh, green chilli.

4 Heat the oil in a large frying pan and fry the onion for 5 minutes until softened, but not coloured. Add the turmeric.

5 Add the chilli, courgettes and peas and fry over a medium heat for about 5 minutes until the vegetables have softened.

6 Stir in the fish, lemon juice, hoisin sauce and water. Bring to the boil, then simmer for about 5 minutes, or until the fish is tender. Season to taste.

7 Drain the pasta thoroughly and turn it into a serving bowl. Toss in the sauce to coat. Serve at once, garnished with fresh dill.

Seafood Laska

For a special occasion serve creamy rice noodles in a spicy, coconut-flavoured broth, topped with a selection of seafood. There is a fair amount of work involved in the preparation, but you can make the soup base ahead.

Serves 4

4 fresh red chillies, seeded and
    roughly chopped
1 onion, roughly chopped
1 piece blacan, the size of a stock cube
1 lemon grass stalk, chopped
1 small piece fresh root ginger,
    roughly chopped
6 macadamia nuts or almonds
60ml/4 tbsp vegetable oil
5ml/1 tsp paprika
5ml/1 tsp ground turmeric
475ml/16fl oz/2 cups stock or water
600ml/1 pint/2½ cups coconut milk
fish sauce (see method)
12 raw king prawns, peeled and deveined
8 scallops
225g/8oz prepared squid, cut into rings
350g/12oz rice vermicelli or rice noodles,
    soaked in warm water until soft
salt and freshly ground black pepper
lime halves, to serve

For the garnish
¼ cucumber, cut into matchsticks
2 fresh red chillies, seeded and
    finely sliced
30ml/2 tbsp mint leaves
30ml/2 tbsp fried shallots

COOK'S TIP

Blacan is dried shrimp or prawn paste. It is sold in small blocks and you will find it in oriental supermarkets.

---

1 In a blender or food processor, process the chillies, onion, blacan, lemon grass, ginger and nuts until smooth in texture.

2 Heat 45ml/3 tbsp of the oil in a large saucepan. Add the chilli paste and fry for 6 minutes. Stir in the paprika and turmeric and fry for about 2 minutes more.

3 Add the stock or water and the coconut milk to the pan. Bring to the boil, reduce the heat and simmer gently for 15–20 minutes. Season to taste with the fish sauce.

4 Season the seafood with salt and pepper. Heat the remaining oil in a frying pan, add the seafood and stir-fry quickly for 2–3 minutes until cooked.

5 Add the noodles to the broth and heat through. Divide among individual serving bowls. Place the fried seafood on top, then garnish with the cucumber, chillies, mint and fried shallots. Serve with the limes.

Sweet and Sour Prawns with Egg Noodles

A quick and easy dish full of flavour.

INGREDIENTS

Serves 4–6

15g/½oz dried porcini mushrooms

300ml/½ pint/1¼ cups hot water

bunch of spring onions, cut into thick
  diagonal slices

2.5cm/1in piece fresh root ginger, peeled
  and grated

1 red pepper, seeded and diced

225g/8oz can water chestnuts, sliced

45ml/3 tbsp light soy sauce

30ml/2 tbsp sherry

350g/12oz large cooked prawns, peeled

225g/8oz Chinese egg noodles

1 Put the dried porcini
  mushrooms into a bowl with
the hot water and set aside to soak
for 15 minutes.

2 Put the sliced spring onions,
  grated ginger and diced red
pepper into a pan with the
mushrooms and their liquid. Bring
to the boil, cover and cook for
about 5 minutes until tender.

3 Add the water chestnuts, soy
  sauce, sherry and prawns.
Cover and cook gently over a low
heat for 2 minutes.

4 Cook the egg noodles
  according to the instructions
on the packet. Drain thoroughly
and transfer to a warmed serving
dish. Spoon the hot prawns on top.
Serve at once.

Farfalle with Prawns

Creamy sauces are not invariably the best way to serve fish with pasta. This simple, fresh prawn sauce allows the distinctive flavour of the fish to be identified.

INGREDIENTS

Serves 4

225g/8oz fresh or dried farfalle
    (pasta bows)
350g/12oz raw or cooked prawns
115g/4oz unsalted butter
2 garlic cloves, crushed
45ml/3 tbsp chopped fresh parsley
salt and freshly ground black pepper

1 If using fresh pasta, cook in boiling, salted water for 2–3 minutes, or until tender but still firm to the bite. Cook dried pasta according to the packet instructions. Peel and devein the prawns.

2 Heat the butter in a large, heavy-based saucepan with the garlic and parsley. Toss in the prawns and sauté for 8 minutes (for cooked prawns 4 minutes will be sufficient).

3 Drain the pasta thoroughly and rinse with boiling water to remove any starch.

4 Stir the pasta into the prawn mixture. Season with salt and pepper to taste and serve.

Bamie Goreng

This fried noodle dish from Indonesia is wonderfully accommodating. To the basic recipe you can add other vegetables, such as mushrooms, broccoli, leeks or beansprouts, if you prefer. You can use whatever you have to hand, bearing in mind the importance of achieving a balance of colours, flavours and textures.

INGREDIENTS

Serves 6–8

450g/1lb dried egg noodles
1 boneless, skinless chicken breast
115g/4oz pork fillet
115g/4oz calves' liver (optional)
2 eggs, beaten
90ml/6 tbsp oil
25g/1oz butter or margarine
2 garlic cloves, crushed
115g/4oz cooked peeled prawns
115g/4oz spinach or Chinese leaves
2 celery sticks, finely sliced
4 spring onions, shredded
about 60ml/4 tbsp chicken stock
dark soy sauce and light soy sauce
salt and freshly ground black pepper
deep-fried onions and celery leaves,
    to garnish
mixed fruit and vegetable salad, to
    serve (optional)

1 Cook the noodles in lightly salted, boiling water for 3–4 minutes. Drain, rinse with cold water and drain well again. Set aside until required.

2 Finely slice the chicken, pork fillet and calves' liver, if using.

3 Season the eggs. Heat 5ml/ 1 tsp of the oil with the butter or margarine in a small pan until melted. Stir in the eggs and keep stirring until scrambled. Set aside.

4 Heat the remaining oil in a preheated wok and stir-fry the garlic with the chicken, pork and liver for 2–3 minutes, until they have changed colour. Stir in the prawns, spinach or Chinese leaves, celery and spring onions.

5 Add the drained noodles and toss the mixture well so that all the ingredients are thoroughly combined. Add just enough stock to moisten and add dark and light soy sauce to taste. Finally, stir in the scrambled eggs.

6 Garnish the dish with deep-fried onions and celery leaves. Serve with a mixed fruit and vegetable salad, if liked.

Buckwheat Noodles with Smoked Trout

The light, crisp texture of the pak choi balances the strong, earthy flavours of the mushrooms, the buckwheat noodles and the smokiness of the trout.

Serves 4

350g/12oz buckwheat noodles
30ml/2 tbsp vegetable oil
115g/4oz fresh shiitake mushrooms,
    quartered
2 garlic cloves, finely chopped
15ml/1 tbsp grated fresh root ginger
225g/8oz pak choi
1 spring onion, finely sliced diagonally
15ml/1 tbsp dark sesame oil
30ml/2 tbsp mirin
30ml/2 tbsp soy sauce
2 smoked trout, skinned and boned
salt and freshly ground black pepper
30ml/2 tbsp coriander leaves and 10ml/
    2 tsp sesame seeds, toasted, to garnish

1 Cook the buckwheat noodles in a saucepan of boiling water for about 7–10 minutes, or until just tender, according to the packet instructions.

2 Meanwhile, heat the oil in a large frying pan. Add the shiitake mushrooms and sauté over a medium heat for 3 minutes. Add the garlic, ginger and pak choi, and continue to sauté for a further 2 minutes.

3 Drain the noodles and add them to the mushroom mixture, with the spring onion, sesame oil, mirin and soy sauce. Toss and season with salt and pepper to taste.

4 Break up the trout into bite-sized pieces. Arrange the noodle mixture on individual serving plates and top with trout.

5 Garnish the noodles with coriander leaves and sesame seeds and serve immediately.

COOK'S TIP
~
Mirin is sweet, cooking sake, available from Japanese stores.

Stir-fried Noodles with Sweet Salmon

A delicious sauce forms the marinade for the salmon in this recipe. Served with soft-fried noodles, it makes a stunning dish.

INGREDIENTS

Serves 4

350g/12oz salmon fillet

30ml/2 tbsp Japanese soy sauce (shoyu)

30ml/2 tbsp sake

60ml/4 tbsp mirin or sweet sherry

5ml/1 tsp light brown soft sugar

10ml/2 tsp grated fresh root ginger

3 cloves garlic, 1 crushed, and 2 sliced into rounds

30ml/2 tbsp groundnut oil

225g/8oz dried egg noodles, cooked and drained

50g/2oz alfalfa sprouts

30ml/2 tbsp sesame seeds, lightly toasted

1 Thinly slice the salmon, then place in a shallow dish.

2 In a bowl, mix together the soy sauce, sake, mirin or sherry, sugar, ginger and crushed garlic. Pour over the salmon, cover and leave to marinate for 30 minutes.

3 Drain the salmon, scraping off and reserving the marinade. Place the salmon in a single layer on a baking sheet. Cook under a preheated grill for 2–3 minutes, without turning.

4 Meanwhile, heat a wok until hot, add the oil and swirl it around. Add the garlic rounds and cook until golden brown, but do not allow them to burn.

5 Add the cooked noodles and reserved marinade to the wok. Stir-fry for 3–4 minutes, until the marinade has reduced slightly to make a syrupy glaze that coats the egg noodles.

6 Toss in the alfalfa sprouts, then remove immediately from the heat. Transfer to warmed serving plates and top with the salmon. Sprinkle over the toasted sesame seeds. Serve at once.

COOK'S TIP

It is important to scrape the marinade off the fish as any remaining pieces of ginger or garlic would burn during grilling and spoil the finished dish.

Smoked Trout Cannelloni

*Smoked trout can be bought already
filleted or as whole fish. They make
a delicious change from the tomato-
based fillings usually found in
cannelloni dishes.*

INGREDIENTS

Serves 4-6
1 large onion, finely chopped
1 garlic clove, crushed
60ml/4 tbsp vegetable stock
2 x 400g/14oz cans chopped tomatoes
2.5ml/½ tsp dried mixed herbs
1 smoked trout, weighing about
    400g/14oz or 225g/8oz of fillets
75g/3oz frozen peas, thawed
75g/3oz fresh breadcrumbs
16 cannelloni tubes, cooked
salt and freshly ground black pepper
mixed salad, to serve

For the cheese sauce
30ml/2 tbsp butter or margarine
25g/1oz flour
350ml/12fl oz/1½ cups skimmed milk
freshly grated nutmeg
25ml/1½ tbsp freshly grated
    Parmesan cheese

1 Simmer the onion, garlic clove
and stock in a large, covered
saucepan for 3 minutes. Uncover
and continue to cook, stirring
occasionally, until the stock has
reduced entirely.

2 Stir in the tomatoes and dried
herbs. Simmer uncovered for a
further 10 minutes, or until the
mixture is very thick.

COOK'S TIP

You can use a 200g/7oz can of
tuna in water in place of the
trout, if preferred.

---

3 Meanwhile, skin the smoked
trout with a sharp knife.
Carefully flake the flesh and
discard all the bones. Mix the fish
together with the tomato mixture,
peas, breadcrumbs, salt and freshly
ground black pepper.

4 Spoon the filling into the
cannelloni tubes and arrange
in an ovenproof dish.

5 For the sauce, put the butter
or margarine, flour and milk
into a saucepan and cook over a
medium heat, whisking constantly,
until the sauce thickens. Simmer
for 2–3 minutes, stirring all the
time. Season to taste with salt,
freshly ground black pepper and
grated nutmeg.

6 Pour the sauce over the stuffed
cannelloni and sprinkle with
the grated Parmesan cheese. Bake
in a preheated oven at 190°C/
375°F/Gas 5 for 30–45 minutes, or
until the top is golden and
bubbling and the sauce is cooked
through. Serve with a mixed salad.

Tuna Lasagne

Lasagne does not always have to be made with minced beef!

INGREDIENTS

Serves 6

350g/12oz oven-ready lasagne
15g/½oz butter
1 small onion, finely chopped
1 garlic clove, finely chopped
115g/4oz mushrooms, thinly sliced
60ml/4 tbsp dry white wine (optional)
600ml/1 pint/2½ cups white sauce
150ml/¼ pint/⅔ cup whipping cream
45ml/3 tbsp chopped fresh parsley
2 x 200g/7oz cans tuna, drained
2 canned pimientos, cut into strips
75g/3oz frozen peas, thawed
115g/4oz mozzarella, grated
25g/1oz freshly grated Parmesan cheese
salt and freshly ground black pepper

1 Soak the sheets of lasagne in a bowl of hot water for 3–5 minutes or according to the packet instructions. Drain and rinse with cold water. Lay them on a tea towel, in a single layer, to drain.

2 Melt the butter in a saucepan and gently fry the onion for 2–3 minutes, until soft but not coloured. Add the garlic and mushrooms and cook until they are soft, stirring occasionally.

3 Pour in the wine, if using. Boil for 1 minute. Add the white sauce, cream and parsley and season to taste.

4 Spoon a thin layer of sauce over the base of a 30 x 23cm/ 12 x 9in baking dish. Cover with a layer of lasagne sheets. Flake the tuna. Scatter half of the tuna, pimiento strips, peas and grated mozzarella over the pasta. Spoon one-third of the remaining sauce evenly over the top and cover with another layer of lasagne sheets.

5 Repeat the layers, ending with lasagne and sauce. Sprinkle with the Parmesan. Bake in a preheated oven at 180°C/350°F/ Gas 4 for 30–40 minutes or until bubbling hot and the top is lightly browned. Cut into squares and serve from the baking dish.

Seafood Chow Mein

This basic recipe can be adapted using a range of different items for the 'dressing'.

INGREDIENTS

Serves 4

75g/3oz squid, cleaned

75g/3oz raw prawns

3–4 fresh scallops, prepared

½ egg white

15ml/1 tbsp cornflour paste

250g/9oz egg noodles

75–90ml/5–6 tbsp vegetable oil

50g/2oz mangetouts

2.5ml/½ tsp salt

2.5ml/½ tsp light brown sugar

15ml/1 tbsp Chinese rice wine or
    dry sherry

30ml/2 tbsp light soy sauce

2 spring onions, finely shredded

vegetable or chicken stock, if necessary

few drops sesame oil

1 Open up the squid and, using a sharp knife, score the inside in a criss-cross pattern. Cut the squid into pieces, each about the size of a postage stamp. Soak the squid in a bowl of boiling water until all the pieces curl up. Rinse in cold water and drain.

2 Peel and devein the prawns, then cut each of them in half lengthways.

3 Cut each scallop into 3–4 slices. Mix the scallops and prawns with the egg white and cornflour paste and set aside.

4 Cook the noodles in boiling water according to the packet instructions, then drain and rinse under cold water. Mix with about 15ml/1 tbsp of the oil.

COOK'S TIP

To make cornflour paste, mix 4 parts dry cornflour with about 5 parts cold water until smooth.

5 Heat about 30–45ml/2–3 tbsp of the oil in a preheated wok until hot. Stir-fry the mangetouts and seafood for about 2 minutes, then add the salt, sugar, rice wine or sherry, half of the soy sauce and about half of the spring onions. Blend well and add a little stock, if necessary. Remove and keep warm.

6 Heat the remaining oil in the wok and stir-fry the noodles for 2–3 minutes with the remaining soy sauce. Place in a large serving dish, pour the 'dressing' on top, garnish with the remaining spring onions and sprinkle with sesame oil. Serve hot or cold.

Seafood Rice

This tasty paella-type meal uses a frozen fish mixture that saves lots of preparation time.

INGREDIENTS

Serves 4

30ml/2 tbsp oil

1 onion, sliced

1 red pepper, seeded and chopped

115g/4oz mushrooms, chopped

10ml/2 tsp ground turmeric

225g/8oz rice and grain mix or
    arborio rice

750ml/1¼ pints/3 cups stock, made with a
    pilau-rice stock cube

400g/14oz bag frozen premium seafood
    selection, thawed

115g/4oz frozen large tiger prawns,
    thawed, peeled and deveined

salt and freshly ground black pepper

1 Heat the oil in a deep frying pan and fry the onion until it is starting to soften. Add the chopped pepper and mushrooms and fry for 1 minute.

2 Stir in the turmeric and then the grains. Stir until well mixed, then carefully pour on the stock. Season with salt and pepper, cover with a lid or foil and leave to simmer gently for 15 minutes.

3 Add the seafood selection and the prawns, stir well and turn up the heat slightly to bring the liquid back to the boil. Cover again and simmer for 15–20 minutes more, until the grains are cooked and the fish is hot. Serve the fish immediately.

COOK'S TIP

If you don't like this fish mixture, choose your own – use more prawns and crab sticks, if you prefer, but cut down on the cooking time for the fish.

Fish with Rice

*This Arabic fish dish, Sayadieh, is
very popular in the Lebanon.*

Serves 4–6
juice of 1 lemon
45ml/3 tbsp oil
900g/2lb cod steaks
4 large onions, chopped
5ml/1 tsp ground cumin
2–3 saffron strands, soaked in 30ml/2 tbsp
    hot water
1 litre/1¾ pints/4 cups fish stock
500g/1¼lb basmati or other long grain rice
115g/4oz pine nuts, lightly toasted
salt and freshly ground black pepper
fresh parsley, to garnish

1 Blend together the lemon juice
and 15ml/1 tbsp of the oil in a
shallow dish. Add the fish steaks,
turning to coat, then cover and set
aside to marinate for 30 minutes.

2 Heat the remaining oil in a
large saucepan or flameproof
casserole and fry the onions for
5–6 minutes until softened and
golden, stirring occasionally.

3 Drain the fish, reserving the
marinade, and add to the pan.
Fry for 1–2 minutes on each side
until lightly golden, then add the
cumin, saffron strands and a little
salt and pepper.

4 Pour in the fish stock and the
reserved marinade, bring to
the boil and then simmer very
gently, over a low heat, for
5–10 minutes, until the fish is
nearly done.

5 Transfer the fish to a plate and
add the rice to the stock. Bring
to the boil, then reduce the heat
and simmer very gently over a low
heat for 15 minutes until nearly all
the stock has been absorbed.

6 Arrange the fish on the rice
and cover. Steam over a low
heat for another 15–20 minutes.

7 Transfer the fish to a plate,
then spoon the rice on to a
large flat dish and arrange the fish
on top. Sprinkle with lightly
toasted pine nuts and garnish with
fresh parsley.

COOK'S TIP

Take care when cooking the rice
that the saucepan does not boil
dry. Check it occasionally and
add more stock or water, if it
becomes necessary.

Salmon Risotto

Any rice can be used for risotto, although the creamiest ones are made with short grain arborio and carnaroli rice. Fresh tarragon and cucumber combine well to bring out the flavour of the salmon.

INGREDIENTS

Serves 4

25g/1oz butter
1 small bunch spring onions, white part
   only, chopped
½ cucumber, peeled, seeded and chopped
400g/14oz short grain arborio or
   carnaroli rice
900ml/1½ pints/3¾ cups chicken or
   fish stock
150ml/¼ pint/⅔ cup dry white wine
450g/1lb salmon fillet, skinned and diced
45ml/3 tbsp chopped fresh tarragon

1 Heat the butter in a large saucepan and add the spring onions and cucumber. Cook for 2–3 minutes without colouring.

2 Add the rice, chicken or fish stock and wine, bring to the boil and simmer, uncovered, for 10 minutes, stirring occasionally.

3 Stir in the diced salmon and chopped tarragon. Continue cooking for a further 5 minutes, then switch off the heat. Cover the pan and leave to stand for 5 minutes before serving.

VARIATION

Long grain rice can also be used. Choose grains that have not been pre-cooked and reduce the stock to 750ml/1¼ pints/3 cups per 400g/14oz of rice.

Truffle and Lobster Risotto

To capture the precious qualities of the fresh truffle, partner it with lobster and serve in a silky smooth arborio. Both truffle shavings and truffle oil are added towards the end of cooking to preserve their flavour.

INGREDIENTS

Serves 4

50g/2oz unsalted butter

1 medium onion, chopped

400g/14oz arborio or carnaroli rice

1 sprig thyme

1.2 litres/2 pints/5 cups chicken stock

150ml/¼ pint/⅔ cup dry white wine

1 freshly cooked lobster

45ml/3 tbsp chopped fresh parsley
   and chervil

3–4 drops truffle oil

2 hard-boiled eggs, shelled and sliced

1 fresh black or white truffle, shaved

1 Melt the butter in a large shallow pan, add the onion and fry gently until soft without letting it colour. Add the rice and thyme and stir well to coat evenly with butter. Pour in the chicken stock and wine, stir once and cook, uncovered, for 15 minutes.

2 Twist off the lobster tail, cut open the underside with scissors and remove the white tail meat. Slice half of the meat, then roughly chop the remainder. Break open the claws with a small hammer and remove the flesh, in one piece if possible.

3 Remove the rice from the heat, stir in the chopped lobster meat, herbs and truffle oil. Cover and leave to stand for 5 minutes.

4 Divide among warmed dishes and arrange the lobster and hard-boiled egg slices and truffle shavings on top. Serve at once.

Rice Layered with Prawns

This dish makes a meal in itself, requiring only pickles or raita as an accompaniment.

INGREDIENTS

Serves 4–6

2 large onions, finely sliced and deep-fried
300ml/½ pint/1¼ cups natural yogurt
25ml/1½ tbsp tomato purée
60ml/4 tbsp green masala paste
25ml/1½ tbsp lemon juice
5ml/1 tsp black cumin seeds
5cm/2in piece cinnamon stick or 1.5ml/
  ¼ tsp cinnamon
4 green cardamoms
450g/1lb cooked king prawns, peeled
  and deveined
225g/8oz small button mushrooms
225g/8oz frozen peas, thawed and drained
450g/1lb basmati rice soaked for
  5 minutes in boiled water and drained
300ml/½ pint/1¼ cups water
1 sachet saffron powder mixed in 90ml/
  6 tbsp milk
30ml/2 tbsp ghee or unsalted butter
salt

1 Mix the first 8 ingredients together in a large bowl. Fold in the prawns, mushrooms and peas. Leave to marinate for 2 hours.

2 Grease the base of a heavy pan and add the prawns, vegetables and any marinade juices. Cover with the drained rice and smooth the surface gently until you have an even layer.

3 Pour the water all over the surface of the rice. Make random holes through the rice with the handle of a spoon and pour a little saffron milk into each.

4 Place a few knobs of ghee or butter on the surface and place a circular piece of foil directly on top of the rice. Cover and cook over a low heat for 45–50 minutes. Gently toss the rice, prawns and vegetables together and serve hot.

Spanish Seafood Paella

Paella is also the name of the heavy, cast-iron pan in which this dish is traditionally cooked.

Serves 4

60ml/4 tbsp olive oil

225g/8oz monkfish or cod, skinned and
  cut into chunks

3 prepared baby squid, body cut into rings
  and tentacles chopped

1 red mullet, filleted, skinned and cut into
  chunks (optional)

1 onion, chopped

3 garlic cloves, finely chopped

1 red pepper, seeded and sliced

4 tomatoes, skinned and chopped

225g/8oz arborio rice

450ml/¾ pint/1⅞ cups fish stock

150ml/¼ pint/⅔ cup white wine

75g/3oz frozen peas

4–5 saffron strands soaked in 30ml/2 tbsp
  hot water

115g/4oz cooked peeled prawns

8 fresh mussels in shells, scrubbed

salt and freshly ground black pepper

15ml/1 tbsp chopped fresh parsley,
  to garnish

lemon wedges, to serve

1 Heat 30ml/2 tbsp of the olive oil in a large frying pan and add the monkfish or cod, the squid and the red mullet, if using. Stir-fry for 2 minutes, then transfer the fish to a bowl with all the juices and set aside.

2 Heat the remaining 30ml/ 2 tbsp of oil in the pan and add the onion, garlic and red pepper. Fry for 6–7 minutes, stirring frequently, until the onion and pepper have softened.

3 Stir in the tomatoes and fry for 2 minutes, then add the rice, stirring to coat the grains with oil, and cook for 2–3 minutes. Pour on the fish stock and wine and add the peas, saffron and water. Season well and mix.

4 Gently stir in the fish with all the juices, followed by the prawns and then push the mussels into the rice. Cover and cook over a gentle heat for about 30 minutes, or until the stock has been absorbed but the mixture is still moist.

5 Remove from the heat, keep covered and leave to stand for 5 minutes. Discard any mussels that do not open. Sprinkle the paella with parsley and serve with lemon wedges.

Smoked Trout Pilaff

Smoked trout might seem an unusual partner for rice, but this is a winning combination.

Serves 4

225g/8oz white basmati rice

40g/1½oz butter

2 onions, sliced into rings

1 garlic clove, crushed

2 bay leaves

2 cloves

2 green cardamom pods

2 cinnamon sticks

5ml/1 tsp cumin seeds

600ml/1 pint/2½ cups boiling water

4 smoked trout fillets, skinned

50g/2oz slivered almonds, toasted

50g/2oz seedless raisins

30ml/2 tbsp chopped fresh parsley

mango chutney and poppadoms, to serve

1 Wash the rice thoroughly in several changes of water and drain well. Set aside. Melt the butter in a large frying pan and fry the onions until well browned, stirring frequently.

2 Add the garlic, bay leaves, cloves, cardamom pods, cinnamon sticks and cumin seeds and stir-fry for 1 minute.

3 Stir in the rice, then add the boiling water. Bring back to the boil. Cover the pan tightly, reduce the heat and cook very gently for 20–25 minutes, until the water has been absorbed and the rice is tender.

4 Flake the smoked trout and add to the pan with the almonds and raisins. Fork through gently. Cover the pan and allow the smoked trout to warm in the rice for a few minutes. Scatter over the parsley and serve with mango chutney and poppadoms.

Mixed Fish Jambalaya

Jambalaya, from New Orleans, is not unlike a paella, but much spicier. The name comes from the French word 'jambon', and tells us that the dish was originally based on ham, but you can add many other ingredients of your choice, including fish and shellfish.

INGREDIENTS

Serves 4

30ml/2 tbsp oil

115g/4oz smoked bacon, rinded and diced

1 onion, chopped

2 sticks celery, chopped

2 large garlic cloves, chopped

5ml/1 tsp cayenne pepper

2 bay leaves

5ml/1 tsp dried oregano

2.5ml/½ tsp dried thyme

4 tomatoes, skinned and chopped

150ml/¼ pint/⅔ cup ready-made tomato sauce

350g/12oz long grain rice

475ml/16fl oz/2 cups fish stock

175g/6oz firm white fish (coley, cod, saithe or haddock), skinned, boned and cubed

115g/4oz cooked peeled prawns

salt and freshly ground black pepper

2 chopped spring onions, to garnish

1 Heat the oil in a large saucepan and fry the bacon until crisp. Add the onion and celery and stir until they begin to stick to the base of the pan.

2 Add the garlic, cayenne pepper, herbs, tomatoes and seasoning and mix well. Stir in the tomato sauce, rice and stock and bring to the boil.

3 Gently stir in the fish and transfer to an ovenproof dish. Cover tightly with foil and bake in a preheated oven at 180°C/350°F/Gas 4 for 20–30 minutes, until the rice is just tender. Stir in the prawns and heat through. Serve sprinkled with the spring onions.

Indonesian Pork and Prawn Rice

Nasi Goreng is an attractive way of using up leftovers and appears in many variations throughout Indonesia. Rice is the main ingredient, although almost anything can be added for colour and flavour.

INGREDIENTS

Serves 4–6

3 eggs

60ml/4 tbsp vegetable oil

6 shallots, or 1 large onion, chopped

2 garlic cloves, crushed

2.5cm/1in piece fresh root
    ginger, chopped

2–3 small red chillies, seeded and
    finely chopped

15ml/1 tbsp tamarind sauce

1cm/½in square piece shrimp paste or
    15ml/1 tbsp fish sauce

2.5ml/½ tsp turmeric

30ml/2 tbsp unsweetened cream of coconut

juice of 2 limes

10ml/2 tsp sugar

350g/12oz lean pork or chicken breasts,
    skinned and sliced

350g/12oz raw or cooked prawn
    tails, peeled

175g/6oz bean sprouts

175g/6oz Chinese leaves, shredded

175g/6oz frozen peas, thawed

250g/9oz long grain rice, cooked

salt

1 small bunch coriander or basil, roughly
    chopped, to garnish

1 In a bowl, beat the eggs with a pinch of salt. Heat a non-stick frying pan over a moderate heat. Pour in the eggs and move the pan around until they begin to set. When set, roll up, slice thinly, cover and set aside.

2 Heat 15ml/1 tbsp of the oil in a preheated wok and fry the shallots or onion until evenly browned. Remove from the wok, set aside and keep warm.

3 Heat the remaining 45ml/ 3 tbsp of oil in the wok, add the garlic, ginger and chillies, and soften without colouring. Stir in the tamarind and shrimp paste or fish sauce, turmeric, cream of coconut, lime juice, sugar and salt to taste. Cook briefly over a moderate heat, stirring constantly. Add the pork or chicken and prawns and fry for 3–4 minutes.

4 Toss the bean sprouts, Chinese leaves and peas in the spice mixture and cook briefly. Add the rice and stir-fry for 6–8 minutes, stirring to prevent it from burning. Transfer to a large serving plate, decorate with shredded egg pancake, the fried shallots or onion, and chopped coriander or basil.

Mixed Smoked Fish Kedgeree

An ideal breakfast dish on a cold morning. Garnish with quartered hard-boiled eggs and season well.

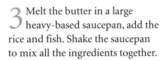

INGREDIENTS

Serves 6

450g/1lb mixed smoked fish such as
   smoked cod, smoked haddock, smoked
   mussels or oysters if available
300ml/½ pint/1¼ cups milk
175g/6oz long grain rice
1 slice lemon
50g/2oz butter
5ml/1 tsp medium curry powder
2.5ml/½ tsp freshly grated nutmeg
15ml/1 tbsp chopped fresh parsley
salt and freshly ground black pepper
2 eggs, hard-boiled, shelled and quartered,
   to serve

2 Cook the rice in salted boiling water, together with a slice of lemon, for 10 minutes, until just cooked. Drain well.

3 Melt the butter in a large heavy-based saucepan, add the rice and fish. Shake the saucepan to mix all the ingredients together.

4 Stir in the curry powder, nutmeg, parsley and seasoning. Serve immediately, garnished with quartered eggs.

1 Put the smoked fish and milk in a pan, cover and poach for 10 minutes, or until it flakes. Drain off the milk and flake the fish. Mix with the smoked seafood.

FRIED AND
GRILLED
DISHES

~

Pan-fried Garlic Sardines

*Lightly fry a sliced clove of garlic to
garnish the fish. This dish could also
be made with sprats or fresh
anchovies, if available.*

INGREDIENTS

Serves 4

1.1kg/2½lb fresh sardines
30ml/2 tbsp olive oil
4 garlic cloves
finely grated rind of 2 lemons
30ml/2 tbsp chopped fresh parsley
salt and freshly ground black pepper

For the tomato bread
2 large ripe beefsteak tomatoes
8 slices crusty bread, toasted

2 Heat the oil in a frying pan
and add the garlic cloves. Cook
until soft.

3 Add the sardines and fry for
4–5 minutes. Sprinkle over the
lemon rind, parsley and seasoning.

4 Cut the tomatoes in half and
rub them on to the toast,
discarding the skins. Serve the
sardines with the tomato toast.

1 Gut and clean the sardines
thoroughly.

Sea Bream with Orange Sauce

Sea bream is a taste revelation to anyone not yet familiar with its creamy rich flavour. The fish has a firm white flesh that scrumptiously partners a rich butter sauce, sharpened here with a dash of frozen orange juice concentrate.

INGREDIENTS

Serves 2

2 x 350g/12oz sea bream, scaled
   and gutted
10ml/2 tsp Dijon mustard
5ml/1 tsp fennel seeds
30ml/2 tbsp olive oil
50g/2oz watercress
175g/6oz mixed salad leaves, such as curly
   endive or frisée
jacket potatoes and orange slices, to serve

For the sauce
30ml/2 tbsp frozen orange
   juice concentrate
175g/6oz unsalted butter, diced
salt and cayenne pepper

1 Slash the bream diagonally four times on either side with a sharp knife. Combine the mustard and fennel seeds, then spread over both sides of the fish. Moisten with oil and cook under a preheated grill for 12 minutes, turning once.

2 Place the orange juice concentrate in a bowl and heat over 2.5cm/1in of boiling water. Remove the pan from the heat and gradually whisk the butter into the juice until creamy. Season, cover and set aside.

3 Moisten the watercress and salad leaves with the remaining olive oil. Arrange the fish on two large plates, spoon over the sauce and serve with the salad leaves, potatoes and orange slices.

COOK'S TIP

For speedy jacket potatoes, microwave small potatoes on 100% high power for 8 minutes, then crisp in a hot oven preheated to 200°C/400°F/Gas 6 for a further 10 minutes. Split, insert butter and serve.

Monkfish with Mexican Salsa

Monkfish is a firm meaty fish; you can use halibut or cod in its place.

Serves 4

675g/1½lb monkfish tail
45ml/3 tbsp olive oil
30ml/2 tbsp lime juice
1 garlic clove, crushed
15ml/1 tbsp chopped fresh coriander
salt and freshly ground black pepper
coriander sprigs and lime slices, to garnish

For the salsa

4 tomatoes, skinned, seeded and diced
1 avocado pear, peeled, stoned and diced
½ red onion, chopped
1 green chilli, seeded and chopped
30ml/2 tbsp chopped fresh coriander
30ml/2 tbsp olive oil
15ml/1 tbsp lime juice

1 To make the salsa, combine all the salsa ingredients and set aside at room temperature for about 40 minutes.

COOK'S TIP

It is important to remove the tough, pinkish-grey membrane covering the monkfish tail before cooking, otherwise it will shrink and toughen the monkfish.

2 Prepare the monkfish. Using a sharp knife, remove the pinkish-grey membrane. Cut the fillets from either side of the backbone. Cut each fillet in half.

3 Mix together the oil, lime juice, garlic, coriander and seasoning in a non-metallic dish.

4 Add the monkfish to the dish. Turn the monkfish several times to coat with the marinade, then cover the dish and leave to marinate at cool room temperature or in the refrigerator for 30 minutes.

5 Remove the monkfish from the marinade and cook under a preheated grill for 10–12 minutes, turning once and brushing regularly with the marinade, until cooked through.

6 Serve the monkfish garnished with fresh coriander sprigs and lime slices and accompanied by the salsa.

Red Snapper with Coriander Salsa

Snapper is a firm fish with little fat and benefits from a sauce with lots of texture and flavour.

Serves 4

4 red snapper fillets, about 175g/6oz each

25ml/1½ tbsp vegetable oil

15g/½oz butter

salt and freshly ground black pepper

For the salsa

1 bunch fresh coriander, stalks removed

250ml/8fl oz/1 cup olive oil

2 garlic cloves, chopped

2 tomatoes, seeded and chopped

30ml/2 tbsp fresh orange juice

15ml/1 tbsp sherry vinegar

coriander sprigs and orange peel,
  to garnish

salad, to serve (optional)

3 Rinse the fish fillets and pat dry, then sprinkle with salt and pepper on both sides. Heat the oil and butter in a large frying pan. When hot, add the fish and cook for 2–3 minutes on each side, or until opaque throughout. Cook the fish in two batches, if necessary.

4 Transfer the fillets to warmed serving plates. Top with a spoonful of salsa. Serve, garnished with coriander and orange peel and with a salad, if liked.

1 To make the salsa, place the coriander, oil and garlic in a food processor or blender. Process until almost smooth. Add the tomatoes and pulse on and off several times; the mixture should be slightly chunky.

2 Transfer the mixture to a bowl. Stir in the orange juice, vinegar and salt to taste, then set the salsa aside.

Fish Steaks with Mustard Sauce

The simplest of dishes, this mustard sauce turns a plain fish into something special.

Serves 4-6

4–6 halibut or turbot steaks, 2.5cm/
　1in thick
50g/2oz butter, melted
salt and freshly ground black pepper
frisée and lemon wedges, to garnish

For the mustard sauce
60ml/4 tbsp Dijon mustard
300ml/½ pint/1¼ cups double or
　whipping cream
2.5ml/½ tsp caster sugar
15ml/1 tbsp white wine vinegar or
　lemon juice

1 Season the fish steaks with salt and pepper. Arrange them on an oiled rack in the grill pan and brush the tops of the steaks with melted butter.

2 Cook under a preheated grill, about 10cm/4in from the heat, for about 4–5 minutes on each side, or until cooked through. Brush with more melted butter, when you turn the steaks.

3 Meanwhile, make the sauce. Combine the ingredients in a saucepan and bring to the boil, whisking constantly. Simmer, whisking, until the sauce thickens. Remove from the heat, set aside and keep warm.

4 Transfer the fish to warmed plates. Spoon over the sauce and serve immediately, garnished with frisée and lemon wedges.

Spiced Fish Baked Thai-Style

Banana leaves make a perfect, natural wrapping for barbecued foods, but if they are not available, you can use foil instead.

INGREDIENTS

Serves 4

4 red snapper or mullet, about 350g/
    12oz each
banana leaves (optional)
1 lime, plus extra slices to serve
1 garlic clove, thinly sliced
2 spring onions, thinly sliced
30ml/2 tbsp Thai red curry paste
60ml/4 tbsp coconut milk

1 Clean the fish, removing the scales, and then cut several deep slashes in the sides of each with a sharp knife. Place each fish on a layer of banana leaves or foil.

2 Thinly slice half the lime and tuck the slices into the slashes in the fish, together with slivers of garlic. Scatter the spring onions over the fish.

3 Grate the rind and squeeze the juice from the remaining half-lime and mix with the curry paste and coconut milk. Spoon the mixture over the fish.

4 Wrap the banana leaves or foil over the fish to enclose them completely. Tie securely with string and cook on a medium-hot barbecue for about 15–20 minutes, turning occasionally. Serve with lime slices.

COOK'S TIP

A large, whole fish can also be cooked this way. A rough guide for cooking whole fish is to allow about 10 minutes per 2.5cm/ 1in thickness.

Trout with Almonds

This simple and quick recipe doubles easily – you can cook the trout in two frying pans or in batches. In Normandy, hazelnuts might be used in place of almonds.

INGREDIENTS

Serves 2

2 trout, about 350g/12oz each, cleaned

40g/1½oz plain flour

50g/2oz butter

25g/1oz flaked or sliced almonds

30ml/2 tbsp dry white wine

salt and freshly ground black pepper

1 Rinse the trout and pat dry. Put the flour in a large polythene bag and season with salt and pepper. Place the trout, 1 at a time, in the bag and shake to coat with flour. Shake off the excess and discard the remaining flour.

2 Melt half the butter in a large frying pan over a medium heat. When it is foamy, add the trout and cook for 6–7 minutes on each side, until golden brown and the flesh next to the bone is opaque. Transfer the fish to warmed plates and keep warm.

3 Add the remaining butter to the pan and cook the almonds until just lightly browned. Add the wine to the pan and bring to the boil. Boil for 1 minute, stirring constantly, until slightly syrupy. Pour or spoon over the fish and serve at once.

St Rémy Tuna

St Rémy is a beautiful village in Provence in the South of France. Herbs, such as thyme, rosemary and oregano, grow wild on the nearby hillside and feature in many of the recipes from this area.

INGREDIENTS

Serves 4

4 tuna steaks, about 175–200g/6–7oz each, 2.5cm/1in thick

30–45ml/2–3 tbsp olive oil

3–4 garlic cloves, finely chopped

60ml/4 tbsp dry white wine

3 ripe plum tomatoes, skinned, seeded and chopped

5ml/1 tsp dried herbes de Provence

salt and freshly ground black pepper

fresh basil leaves, to garnish

fried potatoes, to serve

1 Season the tuna steaks with salt and pepper. Set a heavy frying pan over a high heat until very hot, add the oil and swirl to coat. Add the tuna steaks and press down gently, then reduce the heat to medium and cook for 6–8 minutes, turning once, until just slightly pink in the centre.

2 Transfer the steaks to a serving plate and cover to keep warm.

3 Add the garlic to the pan and fry for 15–20 seconds, stirring constantly, then pour in the wine and boil until it is reduced by half. Add the tomatoes and dried herbs and cook for 2–3 minutes until bubbling. Season with pepper and pour over the fish steaks. Garnish with fresh basil leaves and serve with fried potatoes.

COOK'S TIP

Tuna is often served pink in the middle, rather like beef. If you prefer it cooked through, reduce the heat and cook for an extra few minutes.

Donu's Lobster Piri Piri

Lobster in its shell, in true Nigerian style, flavoured with dried shrimp.

INGREDIENTS

Serves 2–4
2 cooked lobsters, halved
fresh coriander sprigs, to garnish
boiled white rice, to serve

For the piri piri sauce
60ml/4 tbsp vegetable oil
2 onions, chopped
5ml/1 tsp chopped fresh root ginger
450g/1lb fresh or canned
     tomatoes, chopped
15ml/1 tbsp tomato purée
225g/8oz cooked peeled prawns
10ml/2 tsp ground coriander
1 green chilli, seeded and chopped
15ml/1 tbsp ground, dried prawns
     or crayfish
600ml/1 pint/2½ cups water
1 green pepper, seeded and sliced
salt and freshly ground black pepper

3 Stir in the water, green pepper and salt and pepper to taste, bring to the boil and simmer, uncovered, over a moderate heat for about 20–30 minutes, until the sauce is reduced.

4 Add the lobsters to the sauce and cook for a few minutes to heat through. Arrange the lobster halves on warmed serving plates and pour the sauce over each one. Garnish with coriander sprigs and serve with fluffy white rice.

1 Heat the oil in a large, flame-proof casserole and fry the onions, ginger, tomatoes and tomato purée for 5 minutes or until the onions are soft.

2 Add the prawns, ground coriander, chilli and ground, dried prawns or crayfish and stir well to mix.

Spicy Squid

This aromatically spiced squid dish, Cumi Cumi Smoor, is a favourite in Madura, Indonesia and is simple yet utterly delicious. Gone are the days when cleaning squid was such a chore: now they can be bought ready-cleaned and are available from fish shops, market stalls or from the freezer or fish counters of large supermarkets.

INGREDIENTS

Serves 3–4

675g/1½lb squid, cleaned
45ml/3 tbsp groundnut oil
1 onion, finely chopped
2 garlic cloves, crushed
1 beefsteak tomato, skinned and chopped
15ml/1 tbsp dark soy sauce
2.5ml/½ tsp ground nutmeg
6 cloves
150ml/¼ pint/⅔ cup water
juice of ½ lemon or lime
salt and freshly ground black pepper
boiled rice, to serve

1 Cut the squid bodies into ribbons and chop the tentacles. Rinse and drain well.

2 Heat a wok, toss in the squid and stir constantly for 2–3 minutes, by which time the squid will have curled into attractive shapes or firm rings. Lift out and set aside in a warm place.

3 Heat the oil in a clean pan and fry the onion and garlic, until soft and beginning to brown. Add the tomato, soy sauce, nutmeg, cloves, water and lemon or lime juice. Bring to the boil, then reduce the heat and add the squid with seasoning to taste.

4 Cook gently for a further 3–5 minutes, stirring from time to time. Take care not to overcook the squid. Serve hot or warm, with boiled rice.

VARIATION

Try using 450g/1lb cooked, peeled tiger prawns in this recipe. Add them for the final 1–2 minutes.

Mackerel with Mustard and Lemon Butter

Look for bright, firm-looking really fresh mackerel.

INGREDIENTS

Serves 4

4 fresh mackerel, about 275g/10oz each,
   gutted and cleaned
175–225g/6–8oz young spinach leaves

For the mustard and lemon butter
115g/4oz butter, melted
30ml/2 tbsp wholegrain mustard
grated rind of 1 lemon
30ml/2 tbsp lemon juice
45ml/3 tbsp chopped fresh parsley
salt and freshly ground black pepper

1 To prepare each mackerel, cut off the heads just behind the gills, using a sharp knife, then cut along the belly so that the fish can be opened out flat.

2 Place the fish on a board, skin side up, and, with the heel of your hand, press along the backbone to loosen it.

3 Turn the fish the right way up and pull the bone away from the flesh. Remove the tail and cut each fish in half lengthways. Wash and pat dry.

4 Score the skin three or four times, then season the fish. To make the mustard and lemon butter, mix together the melted butter, mustard, lemon rind and juice, parsley and seasoning. Place the mackerel on a grill rack. Brush a little of the butter over the mackerel and grill for 5 minutes each side, basting occasionally, until cooked through.

5 Arrange the spinach leaves in the centre of 4 large plates. Place the mackerel on top. Heat the remaining butter in a small pan until sizzling and pour over the mackerel. Serve at once.

Turkish Cold Fish

Cold fish dishes are appreciated in the Middle East and for good reason – they are delicious! This particular version from Turkey can be made using mackerel, if preferred.

INGREDIENTS

Serves 4

60ml/4 tbsp olive oil

900g/2lb porgy or snapper

2 onions, sliced

1 green pepper, seeded and sliced

1 red pepper, seeded and sliced

3 garlic cloves, crushed

15ml/1 tbsp tomato purée

50ml/2fl oz/¼ cup fish stock, bottled clam
    juice or water

5–6 tomatoes, skinned and sliced or
    400g/14oz can tomatoes

30ml/2 tbsp chopped fresh parsley

30ml/2 tbsp lemon juice

5ml/1 tsp paprika

15–20 green and black olives

salt and freshly ground black pepper

bread and salad, to serve

1 Heat 30ml/2 tbsp of the oil in a large roasting tin or frying pan and fry the fish on both sides until golden brown. Remove from the tin or pan, cover and keep warm.

2 Heat the remaining oil in the pan and fry the onion for 2–3 minutes until softened. Add the peppers and continue cooking for 3–4 minutes, stirring occasion-ally, then add the garlic and stir-fry for 1 more minute.

3 Blend the tomato purée with the fish stock, clam juice or water and stir into the pan with the tomatoes, parsley, lemon juice, paprika and seasoning. Simmer very gently for 15 minutes, stirring occasionally.

4 Return the fish to the pan and cover with the sauce. Cook for 10 minutes, then add the olives and cook for a further 5 minutes or until just cooked through.

5 Transfer the fish to a serving dish and pour the sauce over the top. Allow to cool, then cover and chill until completely cold. Serve cold with bread and salad.

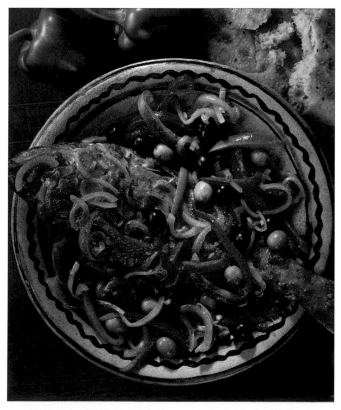

Fish Steaks with Coriander-lime Butter

Citrus-flavoured butter adds just the right kind of zip to fish steaks.

Serves 4

675g/1½lb swordfish or tuna steak,
   2.5cm/1in thick, cut into 4 pieces
60ml/4 tbsp vegetable oil
30ml/2 tbsp lemon juice
15ml/1 tbsp lime juice
salt and freshly ground black pepper
coriander-lime butter (see Cook's Tip)
asparagus and lime slices, to serve

1 Put the fish steaks in a shallow dish. Combine the oil, lemon juice and lime juice, season and pour over the fish. Cover and refrigerate for 1–2 hours, turning the fish once or twice.

2 Drain the fish steaks and arrange on the rack in the grill pan or set over the hot charcoal about 13cm/5in from the coals. Grill for 3–4 minutes, or until the fish is just firm to the touch but still moist in the centre, turning the steaks over once.

3 Transfer to warmed plates and top each fish steak with a pat of coriander-lime butter. Serve the fish immediately with asparagus and slices of lime.

COOK'S TIP

For coriander-lime butter, finely chop 25g/1oz fresh coriander. Mix into 115g/4oz softened, unsalted butter, together with the grated rind and juice of 1 lime. Roll the butter neatly in greaseproof paper and chill in the refrigerator until firm. Other flavoured butters can be made in the same way. Try parsley-lemon butter, made from 30ml/2 tbsp chopped parsley, 115g/4oz unsalted butter and 15ml/1 tbsp lemon juice.

Trout in Wine Sauce with Plantain

Tropical fish would add a distinctive flavour to this Caribbean dish.

INGREDIENTS

Serves 4

15ml/1 tbsp garlic granules
7.5ml/1½ tsp coarse-grain black pepper
7.5ml/1½ tsp paprika
7.5ml/1½ tsp celery salt
7.5ml/1½ tsp curry powder
5ml/1 tsp caster sugar
4 trout fillets
25g/1oz butter
150ml/¼ pint/⅔ cup white wine
150ml/¼ pint/⅔ cup fish stock
10ml/2 tsp clear honey
15–30ml/1–2 tbsp chopped fresh parsley
1 yellow plantain
oil, for frying

1 Mix together the spices and the caster sugar, sprinkle over the trout and marinate for 1 hour.

2 Melt the butter in a frying pan and sauté the fillets for about 5 minutes, until cooked through, turning once. Transfer to a plate and keep warm.

3 Add the wine, fish stock and honey to the pan, bring to the boil and simmer to reduce slightly. Return the fillets to the pan and spoon over the sauce. Sprinkle with parsley and simmer gently for a few minutes.

4 Meanwhile, peel the plantain, and cut into rounds. Heat a little oil in a frying pan and fry the plantain until golden, turning once. Transfer the fish to warmed serving plates, stir the sauce and pour over the fish. Garnish with the fried plantain.

Salmon Cakes with Spicy Mayonnaise

Taste the difference between home-made fish cakes and the inferior store-bought variety with this delicious recipe.

Serves 4

2 boiling potatoes, about 350g/12oz

350g/12oz salmon fillet, skinned and
    finely chopped

30–45ml/2–3 tbsp chopped fresh dill

15ml/1 tbsp lemon juice

flour for coating

45ml/3 tbsp vegetable oil

salt and freshly ground black pepper

spicy mayonnaise (see Cook's Tip) and
    salad leaves, to serve

1 Put the potatoes in a saucepan of boiling salted water and parboil them for 15 minutes.

2 Meanwhile, combine the salmon, dill, lemon juice, salt and pepper in a large bowl.

3 Drain the potatoes and leave them to cool. When they are cool enough to handle, peel away the skins.

4 Shred the potatoes into strips on the coarse side of a grater.

5 Add to the salmon mixture. Mix gently together with your fingers, breaking up the strips of potato as little as possible.

6 Divide the salmon and potato mixture into 8 portions. Shape each into a compact cake, pressing well together. Flatten the cakes to about 1cm/½in thickness.

7 Coat the salmon cakes lightly with flour, shaking off excess.

8 Heat the oil in a large frying pan. Add the salmon cakes and fry for 5 minutes or until crisp and golden brown on both sides.

9 Drain the salmon cakes on kitchen paper and serve with the spicy mayonnaise and salad.

COOK'S TIP

To make spicy mayonnaise, mix together 350ml/12fl oz/1½ cups mayonnaise, 10ml/2 tsp Dijon mustard, 2.5–5ml/½–1 tsp Worcestershire sauce and a dash of Tabasco sauce. You can use home-made or good quality commercial mayonnaise.

Tuna and Corn Fish Cakes

These economical little tuna fish cakes are quick to make. Use fresh mashed potatoes, or make a store cupboard version with instant mash.

INGREDIENTS

Serves 4

300g/11oz cooked mashed potatoes

200g/7oz can tuna fish in soya oil, drained and flaked

115g/4oz canned or frozen sweetcorn

30ml/2 tbsp chopped fresh parsley

50g/2oz fresh white or brown breadcrumbs

salt and freshly ground black pepper

lemon wedges, to garnish

fresh vegetables, to serve

1 Place the mashed potato in a bowl and stir in the tuna fish, sweetcorn and chopped parsley.

2 Season to taste with salt and pepper, then shape into 8 patty shapes with your hands.

3 Spread out the breadcrumbs on a plate and gently press the fish cakes into the breadcrumbs to coat lightly, then transfer to a baking sheet.

4 Cook the fish cakes under a moderately hot grill until crisp and golden brown, turning once. Serve hot with the lemon wedges and fresh vegetables.

COOK'S TIP

For simple store cupboard variations, which are just as nutritious, try using canned sardines, red or pink salmon, or smoked mackerel in place of the tuna fish.

Fresh Tuna Shiitake Teriyaki

Teriyaki is a sweet soy marinade usually used to glaze meat. Here it enhances fresh tuna steaks served with rich shiitake mushrooms.

INGREDIENTS

Serves 4

4 x 175g/6oz fresh tuna or yellowfin
    tail steaks
175g/6oz shiitake mushrooms, sliced
150ml/¼ pint/⅔ cup teriyaki sauce
225g/8oz white radish, peeled
2 large carrots, peeled
salt
boiled rice, to serve

1 Season the tuna steaks with a sprinkling of salt, then set aside for 20 minutes for it to penetrate. Mix together the fish and sliced mushrooms, pour the teriyaki sauce over them and set aside to marinate for a further 20–30 minutes, or longer if you have the time.

COOK'S TIP

You can make your own teriyaki sauce by mixing together 90ml/ 6 tbsp shoyu, 15ml/1 tbsp caster sugar, 15ml/1 tbsp dry white wine and 15ml/1 tbsp rice wine or dry sherry.

2 Drain the tuna, reserving the marinade and mushrooms. Cook the tuna under a preheated moderate grill or on a barbecue for 8 minutes, turning once.

3 Transfer the mushrooms and marinade to a stainless steel saucepan and simmer over a medium heat for 3–4 minutes.

4 Slice the radish and carrots thinly, then shred finely with a chopping knife. Arrange in heaps on 4 serving plates and add the fish, with the mushrooms and sauce poured over. Serve with plain boiled rice.

Whiting Fillets in a Polenta Crust

Polenta is sometimes called cornmeal. Use quick and easy polenta if you can, as it will give a better crunchy coating.

INGREDIENTS

Serves 4

8 small whiting fillets

finely grated rind of 1 lemon

225g/8oz polenta

30ml/2 tbsp olive oil

15ml/1 tbsp butter

30ml/2 tbsp mixed fresh herbs, such as
   parsley, chervil and chives

salt and freshly ground black pepper

toasted pine nuts and red onion, sliced,
   to garnish

steamed spinach, to serve

1 Make 4 small cuts in each fillet to stop the fish curling up when it is cooked.

2 Sprinkle the seasoning and lemon rind over the fish.

3 Press the polenta on to the fillets. Chill in the refrigerator for 30 minutes.

4 Heat the oil and butter in a large frying pan and gently fry the fillets on each side for 3–4 minutes. Sprinkle over the fresh herbs and garnish with toasted pine nuts and red onion slices. Serve immediately with steamed spinach.

Herrings in Oatmeal with Mustard

Oatmeal makes a delicious, crunchy coating for tender herrings.

INGREDIENTS

Serves 4

about 15ml/1 tbsp Dijon mustard
about 7.5ml/1½ tsp tarragon vinegar
175ml/6fl oz/¾ cup thick mayonnaise
4 herrings, about 225g/8oz each, gutted
   and cleaned
1 lemon, halved
115g/4oz medium oatmeal
salt and freshly ground black pepper

1 Beat mustard and vinegar to taste into the mayonnaise. Chill lightly.

2 Place one fish at a time on a board, cut side down and opened out. Press gently along the backbone with your thumbs. Turn over the fish and carefully lift away the backbone.

3 Squeeze lemon juice over both sides of the fish, then season with salt and pepper. Fold the fish in half, skin side outwards.

4 Place the oatmeal on a plate, then coat each herring evenly in the oatmeal, pressing it in gently but firmly.

5 Place the herrings on a grill rack and cook under a preheated moderately hot grill for 3–4 minutes on each side, until the skin is golden brown and crisp and the flesh flakes easily. Serve immediately with the mustard sauce, served separately.

Fish and Chips

This classic British dish is quick and easy to make at home.

INGREDIENTS

Serves 4

115g/4oz self-raising flour
150ml/¼ pint/⅔ cup water
675g/1½lb potatoes
675g/1½lb piece skinned cod fillet, cut
   into 4 pieces
oil, for deep-frying
salt
lemon wedges, to garnish

1 Sift the flour and a pinch of salt together in a bowl, then form a well in the centre. Gradually pour in the water, whisking in the flour to make a smooth batter. Set aside to rest for 30 minutes.

2 Cut the potatoes into strips about 1cm/½in wide and 5cm/2 in long. Place them in a colander and rinse in cold water, then drain and dry well.

3 Heat the oil in a deep-fat fryer or large heavy pan to 150°C/ 300°F. Using the wire basket, lower the potatoes in batches into the oil and cook for 5–6 minutes, shaking the basket occasionally until the potatoes are soft but not browned. Remove the chips from the oil and drain thoroughly on kitchen paper.

4 Heat the oil in the fryer to 190°C/375°F. Season the fish. Stir the batter, then dip the pieces of fish into it, in turn, allowing the excess to drain off.

5 Working in two batches if necessary, lower the fish into the oil and fry for 6–8 minutes, until crisp and golden brown. Drain the fish on kitchen paper and keep warm.

6 Add the chips in batches to the oil and cook for 2–3 minutes, until golden brown and crisp. Keep hot. Sprinkle with salt and serve with the fish, garnished with lemon wedges.

Cod with Caper Sauce

This quick and easy sauce, with a slightly sharp and 'nutty' flavour, is a very effective way of enhancing rather bland fish.

Serves 4

4 cod steaks, about 175g/6oz each

115g/4oz butter

15ml/1 tbsp vinegar

15ml/1 tbsp capers

15ml/1 tbsp chopped fresh parsley

salt and freshly ground black pepper

tarragon sprigs, to garnish

1 Season the cod with salt and pepper to taste. Melt 25g/1oz of the butter, then brush some over one side of each piece of cod.

2 Cook the cod under a preheated grill for about 6 minutes, turn it over, brush with more melted butter and cook for a further 5–6 minutes, or until the fish flakes easily.

3 Meanwhile, heat the remaining butter until it turns golden brown, but do not allow it to burn. Add the vinegar, followed by the capers, and stir well.

4 Pour the vinegar, butter and capers over the fish, sprinkle with parsley and garnish with the tarragon sprigs.

COOK'S TIP

Thick tail fillets of cod or haddock could be used in place of the cod steaks, if you prefer.

Cod with Spiced Red Lentils

This delicious dish marries the spices of India with the delicate flavour of cod.

INGREDIENTS

Serves 4

175g/6oz red lentils
1.5ml/¼ tsp ground turmeric
600ml/1 pint/2½ cups fish stock
30ml/2 tbsp vegetable oil
7.5ml/1½ tsp cumin seeds
15ml/1 tbsp grated fresh root ginger
2.5ml/½ tsp cayenne pepper
15ml/1 tbsp lemon juice
30ml/2 tbsp chopped fresh coriander
450g/1lb cod fillets, skinned and cut into
    large chunks
salt
coriander leaves and 4–8 lemon wedges,
    to garnish

1 Put the lentils in a pan with the turmeric and stock. Bring to the boil, cover and simmer for 20–25 minutes, until the lentils are just tender. Remove from the heat and add salt to taste.

2 Heat the oil in a small frying pan. Add the cumin seeds and, when they begin to pop, add the ginger and cayenne pepper. Stir-fry the spices for a few seconds, then pour on to the lentils. Add the lemon juice and the chopped coriander and stir in gently.

3 Lay the pieces of cod on top of the lentils, cover the pan and then cook gently over a low heat for about 10–15 minutes, until the fish is tender.

4 Transfer the lentils and cod to warmed serving plates. Sprinkle over the coriander leaves and garnish each serving with 1–2 lemon wedges. Serve hot.

Fish Fillets with Orange and Tomato Sauce

Citrus flavours liven up any plain white fish beautifully.

Serves 4

45ml/3 tbsp plain flour

4 fillets of firm white fish, such as cod, sea
    bass or sole, about 675g/1½lb

15g/½oz butter or margarine

30ml/2 tbsp olive oil

1 onion, sliced

2 garlic cloves, chopped

1.5ml/¼ tsp ground cumin

500g/1¼lb tomatoes, skinned, seeded and
    chopped, or 400g/14oz canned
    chopped tomatoes

120ml/4fl oz/½ cup fresh orange juice

salt and freshly ground black pepper

orange wedges, for garnishing

1 Put the flour on a plate and season well with salt and pepper. Coat the fish fillets lightly with the seasoned flour, shaking off any excess.

2 Heat the butter or margarine and half the oil in a large frying pan. Add the fish fillets to the pan and cook for about 3 minutes on each side, until golden brown and the flesh flakes easily when tested with a fork.

3 When the fish is cooked, transfer to a warmed serving platter. Cover with foil and keep warm while you make the sauce.

4 Heat the remaining oil in the pan. Add the onion and garlic and cook for about 5 minutes, until softened but not coloured.

5 Stir in the ground cumin, tomatoes and orange juice. Bring to the boil and cook, stirring frequently, for about 10 minutes, until thickened.

6 Garnish the fish with orange wedges and serve immediately, passing the sauce separately.

Cajun-style Cod

This recipe works equally well with any firm-fleshed fish, such as swordfish, shark, tuna or halibut.

Serves 4

4 cod steaks, each weighing about
    175g/6oz
30ml/2 tbsp plain yogurt
15ml/1 tbsp lime or lemon juice
1 garlic clove, crushed
5ml/1 tsp ground cumin
5ml/1 tsp paprika
5ml/1 tsp mustard powder
2.5ml/½ tsp cayenne powder
2.5ml/½ tsp dried thyme
2.5ml/½ tsp oregano
vegetable oil, for brushing
baby potatoes and mixed salad, to serve

1 Pat the fish dry on absorbent kitchen paper. Mix together the yogurt and lime or lemon juice and brush lightly over both sides of the fish.

2 Mix together the garlic, cumin, paprika, mustard powder, cayenne, thyme and oregano. Coat both sides of the fish with the seasoning mix, rubbing in well.

3 Brush a ridged grill pan or heavy-based frying pan with a little oil. Heat until very hot. Add the fish and cook over a high heat for 4 minutes, or until the underside is well browned.

4 Brush the fish with a little more oil, if necessary, turn over and cook for a further 4 minutes, or until the steaks have cooked through. Serve at once, accompanied with baby potatoes and a mixed salad.

Monkfish with Peppered Citrus Marinade

Monkfish is a firm, meaty fish that cooks well on the barbecue and keeps its shape.

INGREDIENTS

Serves 4

2 monkfish tails, about 350g/12oz each

1 lime

1 lemon

2 oranges

handful of fresh thyme sprigs

30ml/2 tbsp olive oil

15ml/1 tbsp mixed peppercorns, roughly crushed

salt and freshly ground black pepper

lemon and lime wedges, to serve

3 Cut 2 slices each from the lime, lemon and 1 orange and arrange them over 2 of the fillets. Add a few sprigs of thyme and sprinkle with salt and pepper. Finely grate the rind from the remaining fruit and sprinkle it over the fish.

5 Squeeze the juice from the remaining lime, lemon and oranges and mix it with the oil and more salt and pepper. Spoon over the fish. Cover and leave to marinate for about 1 hour, turning occasionally and spooning the marinade over it.

1 Remove any skin from the monkfish tails. Cut carefully down one side of the backbone, sliding the knife between the bone and flesh, to remove the fillet on one side. You can ask your fishmonger to do this for you.

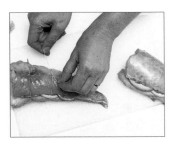

4 Lay the remaining 2 fish fillets on top and tie them firmly with fine cotton string to hold them in shape. Arrange them in a wide dish.

6 Drain the monkfish, reserving the marinade, and sprinkle with the crushed peppercorns. Cook on a medium-hot barbecue for 15–20 minutes, basting it with the marinade and turning it occasionally, until it is evenly cooked through. Serve with lemon and lime wedges.

VARIATION

You can also use this marinade for monkfish kebabs.

2 Turn the fish and repeat on the other side, to remove the second fillet. Repeat on the second tail. Lay the 4 fillets out flat.

Haddock with Parsley Sauce

As the fish has to be kept warm while the sauce is being made, take care not to overcook it.

Serves 4

4 haddock fillets, about 175g/6oz each
50g/2oz butter
150ml/¼ pint/⅔ cup milk
150ml/¼ pint/⅔ cup fish stock
1 bay leaf
20ml/4 tsp plain flour
60ml/4 tbsp double cream
1 egg yolk
45ml/3 tbsp chopped fresh parsley
grated rind and juice of ½ lemon
salt and freshly ground black pepper
boiled new potatoes and sliced carrots,
    to serve

1 Place the fish in a frying pan, add half the butter, the milk, fish stock, bay leaf and seasoning, and heat over a medium heat to simmering point. Lower the heat, cover the pan and poach the fish for 10–15 minutes, depending on the thickness of the fillets, until the fish is tender and the flesh just begins to flake.

2 Carefully transfer the fish to a warmed serving plate, cover and keep warm while you make the sauce. Return the cooking liquid to a medium heat and bring to the boil, stirring. Simmer for about 4 minutes, then remove and discard the bay leaf.

3 Melt the remaining butter in a saucepan, stir in the flour and cook, stirring, for 1 minute. Remove from the heat and gradually stir in the fish cooking liquid. Return to the heat and bring to the boil, stirring constantly. Simmer for about 4 minutes, stirring frequently.

4 Remove the pan from the heat, blend the cream into the egg yolk, then stir into the sauce with the parsley. Reheat gently, stirring, for a few minutes.

5 Remove from the heat, add the lemon juice and rind and season to taste. Pour into a sauceboat. Serve the fish with the sauce, new potatoes and carrots.

Fish with Lemon, Red Onions and Coriander

A rich mixture of flavours, textures and colours – and all produced in just one pan!

INGREDIENTS

Serves 4

4 halibut or cod steaks or cutlets, about 175g/6oz each

juice of 1 lemon

5ml/1 tsp garlic granules

5ml/1 tsp paprika

5ml/1 tsp ground cumin

4ml/¾ tsp dried tarragon

about 60ml/4 tbsp olive oil

flour, for dusting

300ml/½ pint/1¼ cups fish stock

2 fresh red chillies, seeded and finely chopped

30ml/2 tbsp chopped fresh coriander

1 red onion, cut into rings

salt and freshly ground black pepper

1 Place the fish in a shallow, non-metallic bowl and mix together the lemon juice, garlic, paprika, cumin, tarragon and a little salt and pepper. Spoon the lemon mixture over the fish, cover loosely with clear film and allow to marinate for a few hours or overnight in the refrigerator.

2 Gently heat 45ml/3 tbsp of the oil in a large, non-stick frying pan. Dust the fish with flour, then fry for a few minutes on each side, until golden brown all over.

3 Pour the fish stock around the fish, cover and simmer for about 5 minutes, until the fish is thoroughly cooked through.

4 Add the chopped red chillies and 15ml/1 tbsp of the coriander to the pan. Simmer for a further 5 minutes.

5 Transfer the fish and sauce to a serving plate and keep warm.

6 Meanwhile, heat the remaining olive oil and stir-fry the onion rings until speckled brown. Scatter over the fish with the remaining chopped coriander and serve at once.

Marinated Fish

This dish is of Spanish origin and is also very popular throughout the Caribbean.

INGREDIENTS

Serves 4–6

7.5ml/1½ tsp garlic granules
2.5ml/½ tsp coarse-grain black pepper
2.5ml/½ tsp paprika
2.5ml/½ tsp celery salt
2.5 ml/½ tsp curry powder
900g/2lb cod fillet
½ lemon
15ml/1 tbsp spice seasoning
flour, for dusting
oil, for frying
lemon wedges, to garnish

For the sauce
30ml/2 tbsp vegetable oil
1 onion, sliced
½ red pepper, sliced
½ christophene or chayote, peeled and
    seeded, cut into small pieces
2 garlic cloves, crushed
120ml/4fl oz/½ cup malt vinegar
75ml/5 tbsp water
2.5ml/½ tsp ground allspice
1 bay leaf
1 small hot pepper, chopped
15ml/1 tbsp soft dark brown sugar
salt and freshly ground black pepper

2 Cut the fish into 7.5cm/3in pieces and dust with a little flour, shaking off the excess.

3 Heat the oil in a heavy frying pan and fry the fish pieces for 2–3 minutes until golden brown and crisp, turning occasionally.

4 To make the sauce, heat the oil in a heavy frying pan and fry the onion until soft. Add the pepper, christophene or chayote and garlic and stir-fry for 2 minutes. Pour in the vinegar, add the remaining ingredients and simmer gently for 5 minutes. Leave to stand for 10 minutes, then pour over the fish. Serve hot, garnished with lemon wedges.

1 Mix together all the spices. Place the fish in a shallow dish, squeeze over the lemon, then sprinkle with the spice seasoning and pat into the fish. Leave to marinate in a cool place for 1 hour.

Fried Fish with Piquant Mayonnaise

*This sauce makes fried fish just that
extra bit special.*

INGREDIENTS

Serves 4

1 egg

45ml/3 tbsp olive oil

squeeze of lemon juice

2.5ml/½ tsp finely chopped fresh dill
   or parsley

4 whiting or haddock fillets

50g/2oz plain flour

25g/1oz butter or margarine

salt and freshly ground black pepper

mixed salad, to serve

For the mayonnaise

1 egg yolk

30ml/2 tbsp Dijon mustard

30ml/2 tbsp white wine vinegar

10ml/2 tsp paprika

300ml/½ pint/1¼ cups olive or
   vegetable oil

30ml/2 tbsp creamed horseradish

1 garlic clove, finely chopped

25g/1oz finely chopped celery

30ml/2 tbsp tomato ketchup

1 To make the mayonnaise,
blend the egg yolk, mustard,
vinegar and paprika in a mixing
bowl. Add the oil in a thin stream,
beating vigorously with a wire
whisk to blend it in.

2 When the mixture is smooth
and thick, beat in all the other
mayonnaise ingredients. Cover and
chill until ready to serve.

3 Combine the egg, 15ml/1 tbsp
of the olive oil, the lemon
juice, the dill or parsley and a little
salt and pepper in a shallow dish.
Beat until well mixed.

4 Dip both sides of each fish
fillet in the egg and herb
mixture, then coat the fillets lightly
and evenly with flour, shaking off
the excess.

5 Heat the butter or margarine
with the remaining olive oil in
a large, heavy-based frying pan.
Fry the coated fish fillets for
8–10 minutes, until golden brown
on both sides and cooked through.
If necessary, cook the fish in two
batches, keeping the cooked fish
warm while you are cooking
the remainder.

6 Serve the fish hot, with the
piquant mayonnaise and
accompanied by a salad.

Crumb-coated Prawns

Serve these crunchy breaded prawns with a home-made or ready-made dipping sauce of your choice.

Serves 4

90g/3½oz polenta

about 5–10ml/1–2 tsp cayenne pepper

2.5ml/½ tsp ground cumin

5ml/1 tsp salt

30ml/2 tbsp chopped fresh coriander
    or parsley

1kg/2¼lb large raw prawns, peeled
    and deveined

plain flour, for dredging

50ml/2fl oz/¼ cup vegetable oil

115g/4oz coarsely grated Cheddar cheese

lime wedges and tomato salsa or relish,
    to serve

1 Mix the polenta, cayenne pepper, cumin, salt and coriander or parsley in a bowl.

2 Coat the prawns lightly in flour, then dip them in water and roll in the polenta mixture to coat evenly.

3 Heat the oil in a frying pan. When hot, add the prawns, in batches if necessary. Cook for 2–3 minutes on each side, until they are cooked through. Drain on kitchen paper.

4 Preheat the grill. Place the prawns in a baking dish or in 4 individual flameproof dishes. Sprinkle over the cheese. Grill for 2–3 minutes. Serve with lime wedges and tomato salsa or relish.

Sweet and Sour Prawns

It is best to use raw prawns if available. If you are using cooked ones, add them to the sauce without the initial deep-frying.

INGREDIENTS

Serves 4–6

450g/1lb raw king prawns in their shells

vegetable oil, for deep-frying

lettuce leaves, to serve

For the sauce

15ml/1 tbsp vegetable oil

15ml/1 tbsp finely chopped spring onions

10ml/2 tsp finely chopped fresh
    root ginger

30ml/2 tbsp light soy sauce

30ml/2 tbsp soft light brown sugar

45ml/3 tbsp rice vinegar

15ml/1 tbsp Chinese rice wine or
    dry sherry

about 120ml/4fl oz/½ cup chicken or
    vegetable stock

15ml/1 tbsp cornflour paste

few drops sesame oil

1 Pull the soft legs off the prawns without removing the shells. Dry well with kitchen paper.

2 Heat the vegetable oil in a large pan or deep-fryer to 180°C/350°F and deep-fry the prawns for 35–40 seconds, or until their colour changes from grey to bright orange. Remove and drain on kitchen paper.

3 To make the sauce, heat the oil in a preheated wok, add the spring onions and ginger, followed by the seasonings and stock, and bring to the boil.

4 Add the prawns to the sauce, blend well, then thicken the sauce with the cornflour paste, stirring until smooth. Sprinkle with the sesame oil. Serve on a bed of lettuce.

Prawns and Fish in a Herb Sauce

Bengalis are famous for their seafood dishes and always use mustard oil in recipes because it imparts a unique flavour and aroma. No feast is complete without one of these celebrated fish dishes.

INGREDIENTS

Serves 4–6

3 garlic cloves

5cm/2in piece fresh ginger

1 large leek, roughly chopped

4 green chillies

5ml/1 tsp vegetable oil (optional)

60ml/4 tbsp mustard oil

15ml/1 tbsp ground coriander

2.5ml/½ tsp fennel seeds

15ml/1 tbsp crushed yellow mustard seeds
  or 5ml/1 tsp mustard powder

175ml/6fl oz/¾ cup thick coconut milk

225g/8oz huss or monkfish, sliced

225g/8oz raw king prawns, peeled and
  deveined with tails intact

salt

115g/4oz fresh coriander leaves, chopped

green chillies, to garnish

3 Add the ground coriander, fennel seeds, mustard and coconut milk. Gently bring to the boil, then simmer, uncovered, for about 5 minutes.

4 Add the fish and simmer for 2 minutes, then fold in the prawns and cook until the prawns turn a bright orange-pink colour. Season with salt, fold in the coriander leaves and serve hot. Garnish with green chillies.

1 In a food processor, grind the garlic, ginger, leek and chillies to a coarse paste. Add vegetable oil if the mixture is too dry.

2 In a frying pan, heat the mustard oil with the paste until it is well blended. Keep the window open and take care not to overheat the mixture, as any smoke from the mustard oil will sting the eyes and irritate the nose.

Fish and Prawns with Spinach and Coconut

This dish is a truly delightful medley of flavours that complements the fish and prawn mix.

INGREDIENTS

Serves 4

450g/1lb white fish fillets, such as cod
   or haddock
15ml/1 tbsp lemon or lime juice
2.5ml/½ tsp garlic granules
5ml/1 tsp ground cinnamon
2.5ml/½ tsp dried thyme
2.5ml/½ tsp paprika
seasoned flour, for dusting
vegetable oil, for shallow frying
salt and freshly ground black pepper

For the sauce
25g/1oz butter or margarine
1 onion, finely chopped
1 garlic clove, crushed
300ml/½ pint/1¼ cups coconut milk
115g/4oz fresh spinach, finely sliced
225–275g/8–10oz cooked peeled prawns
1 fresh red chilli, seeded and
   finely chopped

1 Place the fish fillets in a shallow bowl and sprinkle with the lemon or lime juice.

2 Blend together the garlic granules, cinnamon, thyme, paprika and salt and pepper to taste. Sprinkle over the fish, cover loosely with clear film and leave to marinate in a cool place or in the refrigerator for a few hours.

3 Meanwhile, make the sauce. Melt the butter or margarine in a large, heavy-based saucepan and fry the onion and garlic for 5–6 minutes, stirring frequently, until the onion is soft.

4 Place the coconut milk and spinach in a separate saucepan and bring to the boil. Cook gently for a few minutes until the spinach has wilted and the coconut milk has reduced a little, then set aside to cool slightly.

5 Blend the spinach mixture in a blender or food processor for 30 seconds and add to the onion, together with the prawns and red chilli. Stir well and simmer gently for a few minutes, then set aside while you cook the fish.

6 Cut the fish into 5cm/2in pieces and dip in the seasoned flour. Heat a little oil in a large frying pan and fry the fish pieces, in batches if necessary, for about 2–3 minutes each side, until golden brown. Drain thoroughly on kitchen paper.

7 Arrange the fish on a warmed serving plate. Gently reheat the sauce and serve separately in a sauceboat or poured over the fish.

Braised Fish in Chilli and Garlic Sauce

This recipe reflects its Chinese origins. When served in a restaurant, the fish's head and tail are usually discarded before cooking and used in other dishes. A whole fish may be used, however, and always looks impressive, especially for formal occasions and dinner parties.

INGREDIENTS

Serves 4–6

1 carp, bream, sea bass, trout, grouper or
    striped mullet, weighing about
    675g/1½lb, gutted
15ml/1 tbsp light soy sauce
15ml/1 tbsp Chinese rice wine or
    dry sherry
vegetable oil, for deep-frying

For the sauce
2 garlic cloves, finely chopped
2–3 spring onions, finely chopped, with
    the white and green parts separated
5ml/1 tsp finely chopped fresh root ginger
30ml/2 tbsp hot bean sauce
15ml/1 tbsp tomato purée
10ml/2 tsp soft light brown sugar
15ml/1 tbsp rice vinegar
about 120ml/4fl oz/½ cup stock
15ml/1 tbsp cornflour paste
few drops sesame oil

1 Rinse and dry the fish. Score both sides of the fish, as deep as the bone, with diagonal cuts about 2.5cm/1in apart. Rub the fish with soy sauce and rice wine or sherry on both sides, then leave to marinate for 10–15 minutes.

2 Heat the oil in a preheated wok and deep-fry the fish for about 3–4 minutes on both sides or until golden brown. Pour off the excess oil, leaving about 15ml/1 tbsp in the wok.

3 Push the fish to one side of the wok and add the garlic, the white part of the spring onions, ginger, hot bean sauce, tomato purée, sugar, vinegar and stock. Bring to the boil and braise the fish in the sauce for 4–5 minutes, turning it over once. Add the green part of the spring onions. Thicken the sauce with the cornflour paste, sprinkle with the sesame oil, and serve immediately.

Tilapia in Fruit Sauce

Tilapia is widely used in African cooking, but can be found in most fishmongers. Yam or boiled yellow plantains are authentic – and very tasty – accompaniments.

INGREDIENTS

Serves 4

4 tilapia, gutted and cleaned
½ lemon
2 garlic cloves, crushed
2.5ml/½ tsp dried thyme
30ml/2 tbsp chopped spring onions
vegetable oil, for shallow frying
flour, for dusting
30ml/2 tbsp groundnut oil
15g/½oz butter or margarine
1 onion, finely chopped
3 tomatoes, skinned and finely chopped
5ml/1 tsp ground turmeric
60ml/4 tbsp white wine
1 fresh green chilli, seeded and
    finely chopped
600ml/1 pint/2½ cups fish stock
5ml/1 tsp sugar
1 medium underripe mango, peeled,
    stoned and diced
15ml/1 tbsp chopped fresh parsley
salt and freshly ground black pepper

1 Place the fish in a shallow bowl, squeeze the lemon juice all over it and gently rub in the garlic, thyme and some salt and pepper. Place some of the spring onion in the cavity of each fish, cover loosely with clear film and leave to marinate for a few hours or overnight in the refrigerator.

2 Heat a little vegetable oil in a large frying pan, coat the fish with flour, then fry the fish on both sides for a few minutes, until golden brown. Remove from the pan to a plate, using a slotted spoon, and set aside.

3 Heat the groundnut oil and butter or margarine in a saucepan and fry the onion for 4–5 minutes, until soft. Stir in the tomatoes and cook briskly for a few minutes.

4 Add the turmeric, white wine, chilli, fish stock and sugar, stir well and bring to the boil, then cover and simmer gently for 10 minutes.

5 Add the fish and cook over a gentle heat for 15–20 minutes, until the fish is cooked through. Add the mango, arranging it around the fish, and cook briefly for 1–2 minutes to heat through.

6 Arrange the fish on a warmed serving plate with the mango and tomato sauce poured over. Garnish with chopped parsley and serve immediately.

Spanish-style Hake

Cod and haddock cutlets will also work well in this recipe.

INGREDIENTS

Serves 4

30ml/2 tbsp olive oil

25g/1oz butter

1 onion, chopped

3 garlic cloves, crushed

15ml/1 tbsp plain flour

2.5ml/½ tsp paprika

4 hake cutlets, about 175g/6oz each

225g/8oz fine green beans, cut into
    2.5cm/1in lengths

350ml/12fl oz/1½ cups fresh fish stock

150ml/¼ pint/⅔ cup dry white wine

30ml/2 tbsp dry sherry

16–20 fresh mussels, cleaned

45ml/3 tbsp chopped fresh parsley

salt and freshly ground black pepper

crusty bread, to serve

1 Heat the oil and butter in a sauté or frying pan, add the onion and cook for 5 minutes, until softened, but not browned. Add the crushed garlic and cook for 1 minute more.

2 Mix together the plain flour and paprika, then lightly dust over the hake cutlets. Push the onion and garlic to one side of the frying pan. Add the hake cutlets to the pan and fry until golden on both sides.

3 Stir in the beans, stock, wine, sherry and seasoning. Bring to the boil and cook for 2 minutes.

4 Add the mussels and parsley, cover and cook for about 5–8 minutes, until all the mussels open. Discard any closed ones.

5 Serve in warmed, shallow bowls, with crusty bread.

Halibut with Tomato Vinaigrette

Sauce vierge, an uncooked mixture of tomatoes, aromatic fresh herbs and olive oil, can either be served at room temperature or, as in this dish, tiède (slightly warm).

INGREDIENTS

Serves 4

3 large, ripe beefsteak tomatoes, skinned,
    seeded and chopped
2 shallots or 1 small red onion,
    finely chopped
1 garlic clove, crushed
90ml/6 tbsp chopped mixed fresh herbs,
    such as parsley, coriander, basil,
    tarragon, chervil or chives
120ml/4fl oz/½ cup extra virgin olive oil
4 halibut fillets or steaks, 175–200g/
    6–7oz each
salt and freshly ground black pepper
green salad, to serve

1 In a medium bowl, mix together the tomatoes, shallots or onion, garlic and herbs. Stir in the oil and season with salt and freshly ground black pepper. Cover the bowl and set aside at room temperature for about 1 hour to allow the flavours to blend.

2 Preheat the grill. Line a grill pan with foil and brush the foil lightly with oil.

3 Season the fish with salt and pepper. Place the fish on the foil and brush with a little extra oil. Grill for 5–6 minutes, until the fish is lightly browned and cooked through.

4 Pour the sauce into a saucepan and heat gently for a few minutes. Serve the fish with the sauce and a green salad.

Seafood Balti with Vegetables

In this dish, the spicy seafood is cooked separately and combined with the vegetables at the last minute to give a truly delicious combination of flavours.

Serves 4

225g/8oz cod
225g/8oz cooked peeled prawns
6 crab sticks, halved lengthways
15ml/1 tbsp lemon juice
5ml/1 tsp ground coriander
5ml/1 tsp chilli powder
5ml/1 tsp salt
5ml/1 tsp ground cumin
60ml/4 tbsp cornflour
150ml/¼ pint/⅔ cup corn oil

For the vegetables
150ml/¼ pint/⅔ cup corn oil
2 medium onions, chopped
5ml/1 tsp onion seeds
½ medium cauliflower, cut into florets
115g/4oz French beans, cut into 2.5cm/
 1in lengths
175g/6oz sweetcorn
5ml/1 tsp shredded fresh root ginger
5ml/1 tsp chilli powder
5ml/1 tsp salt
4 fresh green chillies, sliced
30ml/2 tbsp chopped fresh coriander
lime slices, to garnish

1 Skin the fish and cut into small cubes. Put into a medium mixing bowl, add the prawns and crab sticks and set aside.

2 In a separate bowl, mix together the lemon juice, ground coriander, chilli powder, salt and ground cumin. Pour this over the seafood and mix together thoroughly, using your hands.

3 Sprinkle on the cornflour and mix again until the seafood is well coated. Set to one side in the refrigerator for about 1 hour to allow the flavours to develop.

4 To make the vegetable mixture, heat the oil in a preheated wok or a karahi. Stir-fry the onions and onion seeds until lightly browned.

5 Add the cauliflower, French beans, sweetcorn, ginger, chilli powder, salt, green chillies and fresh coriander. Stir-fry for about 7–10 minutes over a medium heat.

6 Spoon the fried vegetables around the edge of a shallow dish, leaving a space in the middle for the seafood, and keep warm.

7 Wash and dry the wok or karahi, then heat the oil to fry the seafood pieces. Fry the seafood pieces in 2–3 batches, until they turn a golden brown. Remove with a slotted spoon and drain on kitchen paper.

8 Arrange the batches of seafood in the middle of the dish of vegetables and keep warm while you fry the remaining seafood. Garnish with lime slices and serve.

Chunky Fish Balti with Peppers

Try to find as many differently coloured sweet peppers as possible to make this very attractive dish.

Serves 2–4

450g/1lb cod, or any other firm, white fish
7.5ml/1½ tsp ground cumin
10ml/2 tsp mango powder
5ml/1 tsp ground coriander
2.5ml/½ tsp chilli powder
5ml/1 tsp salt
5ml/1 tsp ginger pulp
45ml/3 tbsp cornflour
150ml/¼ pint/⅔ cup corn oil
3 coloured peppers, seeded and chopped
8–10 cherry tomatoes

1 Skin the fish and cut it into small cubes. Put the fish cubes into a large mixing bowl and add the ground cumin, mango powder, ground coriander, chilli powder, salt, ginger pulp and cornflour. Mix together thoroughly, using 2 spoons or your hands, until the fish is well coated.

2 Heat the oil in a preheated wok or karahi. Lower the heat and add the fish pieces, 3 or 4 at a time. Fry for about 3 minutes, turning and moving them constantly.

3 Drain the fish on kitchen paper. Transfer to a serving dish and keep warm while you fry the remaining fish pieces.

4 Add the peppers to the wok or karahi and fry for 2 minutes. They should still be slightly crisp. Drain on kitchen paper.

5 Add the peppers to the serving dish and garnish with the cherry tomatoes. Serve at once.

Chinese-spiced Fish Fillets

*East meets West with this novel twist
on a classic English dish.*

INGREDIENTS

Serves 4

65g/2½oz plain flour

5ml/1 tsp Chinese five-spice powder

8 skinned fillets of fish, such as plaice or
lemon sole, about 800g/1¾lb in total

1 egg, beaten to mix

40–50g/1½–2oz fine, fresh breadcrumbs

groundnut oil, for frying

25g/1oz butter

4 spring onions, cut diagonally into
thin slices

350g/12oz tomatoes, seeded and diced

30ml/2 tbsp soy sauce

salt and freshly ground black pepper

chives and strips of red pepper, to garnish

1 Sift the flour together with the
Chinese five-spice powder and
salt and pepper to taste on to a
plate. Dip the fish fillets first in the
seasoned flour, then in beaten egg
and finally in breadcrumbs.

2 Pour the oil into a large frying
pan to a depth of 1cm/½in.
Heat until it is very hot and
starting to sizzle. Add the coated
fillets, a few at a time, and fry for
2–3 minutes, according to the
thickness of the fillets, until just
cooked and golden brown on both
sides. Do not crowd the pan or the
temperature of the oil will drop
and allow the fish to absorb too
much oil.

3 Drain the fillets on kitchen
paper, then transfer to plates
and keep warm. Pour off all the oil
from the frying pan and wipe it
out with kitchen paper.

4 Melt the butter in the pan and
add the spring onions and
tomatoes. Stir-fry for 1 minute.
Stir in the soy sauce.

5 Spoon the tomato mixture
over the fish and serve at once,
garnished with the chives and
pepper strips.

Salmon with Watercress Sauce

Adding the watercress right at the end of cooking retains much of its flavour and colour.

Serves 4

300ml/½ pint/1¼ cups crème fraîche

30ml/2 tbsp chopped fresh tarragon

25g/1oz unsalted butter

15ml/1 tbsp sunflower oil

4 salmon fillets, skinned and boned

1 garlic clove, crushed

100ml/3½fl oz/scant ½ cup dry white wine

1 bunch watercress

salt and freshly ground black pepper

salad leaves, to serve

1 Gently heat the crème fraîche in a small pan until just beginning to boil. Remove the pan from the heat and stir in half the tarragon. Leave the herb cream to infuse while you cook the fish.

2 Heat the butter and oil in a frying pan, add the salmon and fry for 3–5 minutes on each side. Remove from the pan and keep warm.

3 Add the garlic to the pan and fry for 1 minute, then pour in the wine and let it bubble until reduced to about 15ml/1 tbsp.

4 Meanwhile, strip the leaves off the watercress stalks and chop finely. Discard any damaged leaves. (Save the watercress stalks for soup, if you like.)

5 Strain the herb cream into the pan and cook for a few minutes, stirring until the sauce has thickened. Stir in the remaining chopped tarragon and the watercress, then cook for a few minutes, until wilted but still bright green. Season and serve at once, spooned over the salmon. Serve with salad leaves.

Salmon with Green Peppercorns

A fashionable discovery of nouvelle cuisine, green peppercorns add piquancy to all kinds of sauces and stews. Available pickled in jars or cans, they are great to keep on hand in your store cupboard.

INGREDIENTS

Serves 4

15g/½oz butter

2 or 3 shallots, finely chopped

15ml/1 tbsp brandy (optional)

60ml/4 tbsp white wine

90ml/6 tbsp fish or chicken stock

120ml/1fl oz/½ cup whipping cream

30–45ml/2–3 tbsp green peppercorns in brine, rinsed

15–30ml/1–2 tbsp vegetable oil

4 pieces salmon fillet, 175–200g/ 6–7oz each

salt and freshly ground black pepper

fresh parsley, to garnish

1 Melt the butter in a heavy-based saucepan over a medium heat. Add the shallots and cook for about 1–2 minutes, until just softened but not coloured.

2 Add the brandy, if using, and the white wine, then add the stock and bring to the boil. Boil vigorously to reduce by three-quarters, stirring occasionally.

3 Reduce the heat, then add the cream and half the peppercorns, crushing them slightly with the back of a spoon. Cook very gently for 4–5 minutes, until the sauce is slightly thickened, then strain and stir in the remaining peppercorns. Keep the sauce warm over a very low heat, stirring occasionally, while you cook the salmon fillets.

4 In a large, heavy frying pan, heat the oil over a medium-high heat until very hot. Lightly season the salmon and cook for 3–4 minutes, until the flesh is opaque throughout. To check, pierce the fish with the tip of a sharp knife; the juices should run clear. Arrange the fish on warmed plates and pour over the sauce. Garnish with parsley and serve.

Salmon with a Tarragon Mushroom Sauce

Tarragon has a distinctive aniseed flavour that is good with fish, cream and mushrooms. This recipe uses oyster mushrooms to provide both texture and flavour.

INGREDIENTS

Serves 4

50g/2oz unsalted butter

4 x 175g/6oz salmon steaks

1 shallot, finely chopped

175g/6oz assorted wild and cultivated
   mushrooms, such as oyster
   mushrooms, saffron milk-caps, bay
   boletus or cauliflower fungus, trimmed
   and sliced

200ml/7fl oz/scant 1 cup chicken or
   vegetable stock

10ml/2 tsp cornflour

2.5ml/½ tsp mustard

50ml/2fl oz/¼ cup crème fraîche

45ml/3 tbsp chopped fresh tarragon

5ml/1 tsp white wine vinegar

salt and cayenne pepper

boiled new potatoes and green salad,
   to serve

1 Melt half the butter in a large frying pan, season the salmon and cook over a moderate heat for 8 minutes, turning once. Transfer to a plate, cover and keep warm.

2 Heat the remaining butter in the pan and gently fry the shallot to soften. Add the mushrooms and cook until the juices begin to flow. Add the stock and simmer for 2–3 minutes.

3 Mix together the cornflour and mustard and blend with 15ml/1 tbsp of water. Stir into the mushroom mixture and bring to a simmer, stirring, to thicken. Add the crème fraîche, tarragon, vinegar and salt and pepper to taste.

4 Spoon the mushrooms and sauce over each salmon steak and serve with new potatoes and a green salad.

COOK'S TIP
~

Fresh tarragon will bruise and darken quickly after chopping, so prepare the herb as and when you need it.

Grilled Butterflied Salmon

Ask your fishmonger to bone the salmon for butterflying.

INGREDIENTS

Serves 6–8

25ml/1½ tbsp dried juniper berries

10ml/2 tsp dried green peppercorns

5ml/1 tsp caster sugar

45ml/3 tbsp vegetable oil

30ml/2 tbsp lemon juice

2.25kg/5–5¼lb salmon, scaled, gutted and
   boned for butterflying

salt

lemon wedges and parsley sprigs,
   to garnish

1 Coarsely grind the juniper berries and peppercorns in a spice mill or in a mortar with a pestle. Turn the ground spices into a small bowl and stir in the sugar, oil, lemon juice and salt to taste.

2 Open the salmon like a book, skin side down. Spread the juniper mixture evenly over the flesh. Fold the salmon closed again and place on a large plate. Cover and marinate in the refrigerator for at least 1 hour.

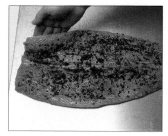

3 Open up the salmon again and place it, skin side down, on an oiled baking sheet. Spoon any juniper mixture left on the plate over the fish.

4 Cook under a preheated grill, about 10cm/4in from the heat, for 8–10 minutes or until the fish is cooked. Serve the fish at once, garnished with the lemon wedges and parsley.

COOK'S TIP

To bone the salmon yourself, follow the instructions for boning a round fish through the stomach. Remove both the head and tail but do not separate the fillets.

Mackerel California-style

Fish, well coated with spices, are often fried until 'blackened' in California, but this does make a lot of smoke and smell in the kitchen. This recipe doesn't go quite that far!

Serves 2–4

10ml/2 tsp paprika

7.5ml/1½ tsp salt

2.5ml/½ tsp onion powder

2.5ml/½ tsp garlic powder

2.5ml/½ tsp white pepper

2.5ml/½ tsp black pepper

2.5ml/½ tsp dried dill

2.5ml/½ tsp dried oregano

2 large, thick mackerel, boned and filleted

115g/4oz butter

lemon slices and oregano, to garnish

1 Mix all the seasonings together. Dip each fillet of mackerel into the spice mixture until well coated.

2 Heat half the butter in a large frying pan until really hot. Add the fish and cook, 2 fillets at a time, for about 2 minutes on each side. Remove immediately, add the rest of the butter and then cook the remaining fillets.

3 Serve piping hot with a little of the butter from the pan poured over and garnished with lemon slices and sprigs of oregano.

COOK'S TIP

Other fish, such as salmon, red snapper and tuna, are also suitable, but thick cuts are best.

Trout with Curried Orange Butter

Small trout are perfect mid-week fare and delicious served with this tangy butter. Children, particularly, like the buttery curry flavour, but it is a good idea to fillet the cooked trout and remove the bones before serving this to very young children.

Serves 4

25g/1oz butter, softened

5ml/1 tsp curry powder

5ml/1 tsp grated orange rind

4 small trout, gutted and heads removed

a little oil

salt and freshly ground black pepper

4 wedges of orange, to garnish

boiled new potatoes, to serve

1 Mix the butter, curry powder, orange rind and seasoning together, wrap in foil and freeze for 10 minutes.

2 Brush the fish all over with oil and sprinkle well with seasoning. Make three diagonal slashes through the skin and flesh, on each side of the fish.

3 Cut the flavoured butter into small pieces and insert into the slashes. Place the fish on the grill tray and cook under a preheated high grill for 3–4 minutes on each side, depending on the thickness. Serve the fish, garnished with wedges of orange, with boiled new potatoes.

PIES AND BAKES

Cod, Basil and Tomato with a Potato Thatch

With a green salad, this makes an ideal dish for a substantial lunch or a family supper.

INGREDIENTS

Serves 8

1kg/2¼lb cod fillet
1kg/2¼lb smoked cod fillet
600ml/1 pint/2½ cups milk
1.2 litres/2 pints/5 cups water
2 basil sprigs
1 lemon thyme sprig
75g/3oz butter
1 onion, chopped
75g/3oz flour
30ml/2 tbsp tomato purée
30ml/2 tbsp chopped basil
12 medium potatoes
50g/2oz butter
300ml/½ pint/1¼ cups milk
salt and freshly ground black pepper
15ml/1 tbsp chopped parsley, to serve

2 Melt the butter in a pan, add the onion and cook for about 5 minutes, until tender but not browned. Add the flour, tomato purée and half the chopped basil. Gradually add the reserved fish cooking liquid, adding a little more milk, if necessary, to make a fairly thin sauce. Bring to the boil, season to taste with salt and pepper, and add the remaining chopped basil. Add the fish carefully and stir gently. Transfer the mixture to an ovenproof dish.

3 Boil the potatoes until tender. Add the butter and milk and mash well. Add salt and pepper to taste and spread over the fish mixture, forking to create a pattern. Bake in a preheated oven at180°C/350°F/Gas 4 for 30 minutes. Serve with the chopped parsley.

1 Place the cod fillet and smoked cod fillet in a roasting tin with the milk, water, basil sprigs and lemon thyme sprig. Simmer over a low heat for about 3–4 minutes. Leave to cool in the cooking liquid for about 20 minutes. Drain the fish, reserving the liquid for use in the sauce. Flake the fish, taking care to remove any skin and bones.

Creamy Fish and Mushroom Pie

Fish pie is a healthy and hearty dish for a hungry family. To help the fish go further, mushrooms provide both flavour and nourishment.

INGREDIENTS

Serves 4

225g/8oz assorted wild and cultivated
    mushrooms, such as oyster, button,
    chanterelle or St George's mushrooms,
    trimmed and quartered
675g/1½lb cod or haddock fillet, skinned
    and diced
600ml/1 pint/2½ cups milk, boiling

For the topping

900g/2lb floury potatoes, quartered
25g/1oz butter
150ml/¼ pint/⅔ cup milk
salt and freshly ground black pepper
grated nutmeg

For the sauce

50g/2oz unsalted butter
1 medium onion, chopped
½ celery stick, chopped
50g/2oz plain flour
10ml/2 tsp lemon juice
45ml/3 tbsp chopped fresh parsley

1 Butter an ovenproof dish, scatter the mushrooms over the base, add the fish and season with salt and pepper to taste. Pour on the boiling milk, cover the dish and cook in a preheated oven at 200°C/400°F/Gas 6 for 20 minutes.

2 Using a slotted spoon, transfer the fish and mushrooms to a 1.5 litre/2½ pint/6¼ cup baking dish. Pour the poaching liquid into a jug and set aside.

3 Meanwhile, cook the potatoes in lightly salted boiling water for 20 minutes. Drain and mash with the butter and milk. Season well with salt, pepper and nutmeg.

4 To make the sauce, melt the butter in a saucepan, add the onion and celery and fry until soft, but not coloured. Stir in the flour, then remove from the heat.

5 Gradually add the reserved liquid, stirring until absorbed. Return to the heat, stir and simmer to thicken. Add the lemon juice and parsley, season, then add to the baking dish.

6 Top with the mashed potato and return to the oven for 30–40 minutes until the topping is golden brown.

Crunchy-topped Cod

Colourful and quick to cook, this is an ideal dish for weekday meals.

INGREDIENTS

Serves 4

4 pieces cod fillet, about 115g/4oz
    each, skinned
2 medium tomatoes, sliced
50g/2oz fresh wholemeal breadcrumbs
30ml/2 tbsp chopped fresh parsley
finely grated rind and juice of ½ lemon
5ml/1 tsp sunflower oil
salt and freshly ground black pepper
vegetables, to serve

2 Arrange the tomato slices on top. Mix together the breadcrumbs, fresh parsley, lemon rind and juice and the oil with seasoning to taste.

3 Spoon the crumb mixture evenly over the fish, then bake in a preheated oven at 200°C/400°F/Gas 6 for 15–20 minutes. Serve hot with vegetables.

1 Arrange the cod fillets in a wide, ovenproof dish.

Special Fish Pie

This fish pie is colourful, healthy and – best of all – very easy to make. For a more economical version, omit the prawns and replace with more haddock fillet.

INGREDIENTS

Serves 4

350g/12oz haddock fillet, skinned
30ml/2 tbsp cornflour
115g/4oz cooked peeled prawns
200g/7oz can sweetcorn, drained
75g/3oz frozen peas
150ml/¼ pint/⅔ cup milk
150g/5oz fromage frais
75g/3oz fresh wholemeal breadcrumbs
40g/1½oz grated Cheddar cheese
salt and freshly ground black pepper
mixed fresh vegetables, to serve

1 Cut the haddock into bite-sized pieces and toss in cornflour to coat evenly.

2 Place the fish, prawns, sweetcorn and peas in an ovenproof dish. Beat together the milk, fromage frais and seasonings, then pour into the dish.

3 Mix together the breadcrumbs and grated cheese, then spoon evenly over the top of the dish. Bake in a preheated oven at 190°C/375°F/Gas 5 for 25–30 minutes, or until golden brown. Serve hot with fresh vegetables.

Golden Fish Pie

Crispy, crunchy filo pastry makes a wonderful contrast to the creamy fish filling.

Serves 4–6

675g/1½lb white fish fillets
300ml/½ pint/1¼ cups milk
2 slices onion
2 bay leaves
6 black peppercorns
115g/4oz cooked peeled prawns, defrosted
    if frozen
115g/4oz butter
50g/2oz plain flour
300ml/½ pint/1¼ cups single cream
75g/3oz Gruyère cheese, grated
1 bunch watercress, leaves only, chopped
5ml/1 tsp Dijon mustard
5 sheets filo pastry
salt and freshly ground black pepper

1 Place the fish fillets in a pan, pour over the milk and add the onion slices, bay leaves and peppercorns. Bring just to the boil, then cover and simmer for about 10–12 minutes, until the fish is almost tender.

2 Remove the fish from the pan with a slotted spoon. Skin and remove any bones, then roughly flake into a shallow ovenproof dish. Scatter the peeled prawns over the fish. Strain the cooking liquid and reserve.

3 Melt 50g/2oz of the butter in a pan. Stir in the flour and cook for 1 minute. Stir in the reserved cooking liquid and the cream. Bring to the boil, stirring, then simmer for 2–3 minutes, until the sauce has thickened.

4 Remove the pan from the heat and stir in the grated Gruyère, watercress, mustard and seasoning to taste. Pour over the fish and set aside to cool.

5 Melt the remaining butter. Brush 1 sheet of filo pastry with a little melted butter, then crumple up loosely and place on top of the filling. Repeat with the remaining filo sheets and butter until they are all used up and the pie is completely covered.

6 Bake in a preheated oven at 190°C/375°F/Gas 5 for 25–30 minutes, until the pastry is golden and crisp.

Cod with Lentils and Leeks

This unusual dish, discovered in a Parisian charcuterie, is great for entertaining. You can cook the vegetables ahead of time and let it bake while the first course is served.

INGREDIENTS

Serves 4

150g/5oz green lentils
1 bay leaf
1 garlic clove, finely chopped
grated rind of 1 orange
grated rind of 1 lemon
pinch of ground cumin
15g/½oz butter
450g/1lb leeks, thinly sliced or cut into
    julienne strips
300ml/½ pint/1¼ cups whipping cream
15ml/1 tbsp lemon juice, or to taste
800g/1¾lb thick, skinless cod or
    haddock fillets
salt and freshly ground black pepper

1 Rinse the lentils and put them in a saucepan with the bay leaf and garlic. Add enough water to cover by 5cm/2in. Bring to the boil and boil gently for 10 minutes, then reduce the heat and simmer for a further 15–30 minutes, until the lentils are just tender.

2 Drain the lentils and discard the bay leaf, then stir in half the orange rind and all the lemon rind and season with ground cumin and salt and pepper. Transfer to a shallow baking dish or gratin dish.

3 Melt the butter in a saucepan over a medium heat, then add the leeks and cook, stirring frequently, until just softened. Add 250ml/8fl oz/1 cup of the cream and the remaining orange rind and cook gently for 15–20 minutes. Stir in the lemon juice and season with salt and plenty of pepper.

4 Cut the fish into 4 pieces and pull out any small bones. Season the fish with salt and pepper, place on top of the lentil mixture and press down slightly into the lentils.

5 Cover each piece of fish with a quarter of the leek mixture and pour 15ml/1 tbsp of the remaining cream over each. Bake in a preheated oven at 190°C/375°F/ Gas 5 for about 30 minutes, until the fish is cooked through and the topping is lightly golden.

Turbot in Parchment

Cooking in parcels is not new, but it is an ideal way to cook fish. Serve this dish plain or with a little hollandaise sauce and let each person open their own parcel to savour the aroma.

INGREDIENTS

Serves 4

2 carrots, cut into thin julienne strips
2 courgettes, cut into thin julienne strips
2 leeks, cut into thin julienne strips
1 fennel bulb, cut into thin julienne strips
2 tomatoes, skinned, seeded and diced
30ml/2 tbsp chopped fresh dill, tarragon, or chervil
4 turbot fillets, about 200g/7oz each, cut in half
20ml/4 tsp olive oil
60ml/4 tbsp white wine or fish stock
salt and freshly ground black pepper

1 Cut 4 pieces of non-stick baking paper, about 45cm/18in long. Fold each piece in half and cut into a heart shape.

2 Open the paper hearts. Arrange one quarter of each of the vegetables next to the fold of each heart. Sprinkle with salt and pepper and half the chopped herbs. Arrange 2 pieces of turbot fillet over each bed of vegetables, overlapping the thin end of one piece and the thicker end of the other. Sprinkle the remaining herbs, the olive oil and wine or stock evenly over the fish.

3 Fold the top half of one of the paper hearts over the fish and vegetables and, beginning at the rounded end, fold the edges of the paper over, twisting and folding to form an airtight packet. Repeat with the remaining three.

4 Slide the parcels on to one or two baking sheets and bake in a preheated oven at 190°C/375°F/Gas 5 for about 10 minutes, or until the paper is lightly browned and well puffed up. Slide each parcel on to a warmed serving plate and serve at once.

Fish Soufflé with Cheese Topping

This is an easy-going soufflé, which will not drop too much if kept waiting. On the other hand, it might be best to get the family seated before you take it out of the oven!

Serves 4

350g/12oz white fish, skinned and boned
150ml/¼ pint/⅔ cup milk
225g/8oz cooked potatoes, still warm
1 garlic clove, crushed
2 eggs, separated
grated rind and juice of ½ small lemon
115g/4oz cooked peeled prawns
50g/2oz grated Cheddar cheese
salt and freshly ground black pepper

1 Place the fish in a large saucepan and add the milk. Bring just to the boil, lower the heat and cook for 12 minutes, or until it flakes easily. Alternatively, place the fish and milk in a bowl and cook in the microwave for 3–4 minutes on high. Drain, reserving the milk, and place the fish in a bowl.

2 Mash the potatoes until really creamy, using as much of the reserved fish milk as necessary. Then mash in the garlic, egg yolks, lemon rind and juice and seasoning to taste.

3 Flake the fish and gently stir into the potato mixture with the prawns. Season to taste.

4 Whisk the egg whites until stiff, but not dry, and gently fold them into the fish mixture. When smoothly blended, spoon into a greased gratin dish.

5 Sprinkle with the cheese and bake in a preheated oven at 220°C/425°F/Gas 7 for about 25–30 minutes, until the top is golden and just about firm to the touch. (If it browns too quickly, reduce the oven temperature to 200°C/400°F/Gas 6.)

Baked Red Snapper

The flesh of the red snapper is made tender and flavourful by rubbing in spices and baking in a sauce.

INGREDIENTS

Serves 3–4

1 large red snapper, gutted and cleaned
juice of 1 lemon
2.5ml/½ tsp paprika
2.5ml/½ tsp garlic granules
2.5ml/½ tsp dried thyme
2.5ml/½ tsp freshly ground black pepper
boiled rice and lemon wedges, to serve

For the sauce

30ml/2 tbsp palm or vegetable oil
1 onion, chopped
400g/14oz can chopped tomatoes
2 garlic cloves, crushed
1 thyme sprig or 2.5ml/½ tsp dried thyme
1 fresh green chilli, seeded and
    finely chopped
½ green pepper, seeded and chopped
300ml/½ pint/1¼ cups fish stock or water

1 Prepare the sauce. Heat the palm or vegetable oil in a saucepan, fry the onion for 5 minutes, then add the tomatoes, garlic, thyme and chilli.

2 Add the pepper and stock or water. Bring to the boil, stirring, then reduce the heat, cover and simmer for about 10 minutes, until the vegetables are soft. Leave to cool a little and then place in a blender or food processor and blend to a purée.

3 Wash the fish well and then score the skin with a sharp knife in a criss-cross pattern. Mix together the lemon juice, paprika, garlic, thyme and black pepper. Spoon the mixture over the fish and rub in well.

4 Place the fish in a greased baking dish and pour the sauce over the top. Cover with foil and bake in a preheated oven at 200°C/400°F/Gas 6 for about 30–40 minutes, or until the fish is cooked and flakes easily when tested with a knife. Serve with boiled rice and lemon wedges.

COOK'S TIP

If you prefer less sauce, remove the foil after 20 minutes and bake, uncovered, until cooked.

Trout Wrapped in a Blanket

The 'blanket' of streaky bacon bastes the fish during cooking, keeping it moist and adding flavour at the same time.

INGREDIENTS

Serves 4

juice of ½ lemon

4 trout, about 275g/10oz each

4 thyme sprigs

8 thin slices streaky bacon, rinds removed

salt and freshly ground black pepper

chopped fresh parsley and thyme sprigs,
    to garnish

lemon wedges, to serve

1 Squeeze lemon juice over the skin and in the cavity of each fish, season all over, then put a thyme sprig in each cavity.

2 Stretch each bacon slice using the back of a knife, then wind 2 slices around each fish. Preheat the oven to 200°C/400°F/Gas 6.

3 Place the fish in a lightly greased, shallow baking dish with the loose ends of bacon tucked underneath to prevent them unwinding.

4 Bake in the preheated oven for about 15–20 minutes, until the trout flesh flakes easily when tested with the point of a sharp knife and the bacon is crisp and is just beginning to brown.

5 To serve, sprinkle the trout with chopped parsley, then garnish with sprigs of thyme and accompany with lemon wedges.

COOK'S TIP

You can partially prepare this dish in advance. The trout can be wrapped in bacon and kept, covered, in the refrigerator until you are ready to cook. Return them to room temperature about 20 minutes before baking.

Stuffed Fish

Every community in India prepares stuffed fish, but the Parsi version must rank top of the list. The most popular fish in India is the pomfret. It is available from Indian grocers or large supermarkets.

INGREDIENTS

Serves 4

2 large pomfrets or Dover or lemon sole
10ml/2 tsp salt
juice of 1 lemon
slices of lime, to serve

For the masala
120ml/8 tbsp desiccated coconut
115g/4oz fresh coriander
8 fresh green chillies (or to taste)
5ml/1 tsp cumin seeds
6 garlic cloves
10ml/2 tsp caster sugar
10ml/2 tsp lemon juice

1 Scale the fish and cut off the fins. Gut the fish and remove the heads, if desired. Using a sharp knife, make 2 diagonal slashes on each side, then pat dry with kitchen paper.

2 Rub the fish inside and out with salt and lemon juice and allow to stand for 1 hour. Pat dry thoroughly with kitchen paper.

3 For the masala, grind all the ingredients together using a pestle and mortar or food processor. Stuff the fish with the masala mixture and rub any remaining masala into the gashes and all over the fish on both sides.

4 Place each fish on a separate piece of greased foil. Tightly wrap the foil over each fish. Place in a steamer and steam for 20 minutes or bake in a preheated oven at 200°C/400°F/Gas 6 for 30 minutes, or until cooked. Serve with slices of lime.

COOK'S TIP

In India, this fish dish is always steamed wrapped in banana leaves. Banana leaves are available from Indian or Chinese grocers, but vine leaves may be used instead.

Baked Fish Creole-style

There is no shortage of fish in Louisiana and cooks there have a wide repertoire of ways of cooking it. This chunky tomato and pepper sauce really livens up plain white fish.

Serves 4

25g/1oz butter, plus extra for greasing
15ml/1 tbsp oil
1 onion, thinly sliced
1 garlic clove, chopped
1 red pepper, seeded, halved and sliced
1 green pepper, seeded, halved and sliced
400g/14oz can chopped tomatoes
15ml/1 tbsp tomato purée
30ml/2 tbsp capers, chopped
3–4 drops Tabasco sauce
4 tail end pieces cod or haddock fillets,
   about 175g/6oz each, skinned
6 basil leaves, shredded
45ml/3 tbsp fresh breadcrumbs
25g/1oz grated Cheddar cheese
10ml/2 tsp chopped fresh parsley
salt and freshly ground black pepper
fresh basil sprigs, to garnish
courgettes and fried potatoes, to serve

1 Butter an ovenproof dish. Heat the oil and half the butter in a pan and add the onion. Fry for about 6–7 minutes, until softened, then add the garlic, red and green peppers, chopped tomatoes, tomato purée, capers and Tabasco sauce and season well. Cover and cook for 15 minutes, then uncover and simmer gently for a further 5 minutes to reduce slightly.

2 Place the fish fillets in the ovenproof dish, dot with the remaining butter and season lightly. Spoon over the tomato and pepper sauce and sprinkle over the shredded basil. Bake in a preheated oven at 230°C/450°F/ Gas 8 for about 10 minutes.

3 Meanwhile, mix together the breadcrumbs, cheese and parsley in a bowl.

4 Remove the fish from the oven and scatter the cheese and breadcrumbs over the top. Return to the oven and bake for a further 10 minutes, until lightly browned.

5 Let the fish stand for about 1 minute, then, using a fish slice, carefully transfer each topped fillet to a warmed serving plate. Garnish with sprigs of fresh basil and serve hot with courgettes and fried potatoes.

Salmon Coulibiac

This is a complicated Russian dish that takes a lot of preparation, but is well worth it. Traditionally sturgeon is used, but, as this is difficult to obtain, salmon may be substituted. As a special treat, serve with shots of chilled vodka for an authentic Russian flavour.

INGREDIENTS

Serves 8

butter, for greasing
flour, for dusting
450g/1lb puff pastry
1 egg, beaten
salt and freshly ground black pepper
lemon wedges and fresh dill sprigs,
    to garnish

For the pancakes
2 eggs, separated
750ml/1¼ pints/3 cups milk
225g/8oz plain flour
350g/12oz butter, melted
2.5ml/½ tsp salt
2.5ml/½ tsp caster sugar

For the filling
50g/2oz butter
350g/12oz chestnut mushrooms, sliced
100ml/3½fl oz/scant ½ cup white wine
juice of ½ lemon
675g/1½lb salmon fillet, skinned
115g/4oz long grain rice
30ml/2 tbsp chopped fresh dill
1 large onion, chopped
4 hard-boiled eggs, shelled and sliced

1 First make the pancakes. Whisk the egg yolks together and add the milk. Gradually beat in the flour, 335g/11½oz of the melted butter, salt and sugar until smooth. Leave to stand for about 30 minutes.

2 Whisk the egg whites until they just form stiff peaks, then fold into the batter. Heat a little of the remaining butter in a heavy-based frying pan and add about 45ml/3 tbsp of the batter. Turn and cook until golden. Repeat until all the mixture has been used up, brushing on a little melted butter when stacking the pancakes. When they are cool, cut into long rectangles, cover and set aside.

3 For the filling, melt most of the butter in a heavy-based frying pan, add the mushrooms and cook for 3 minutes. Add 60ml/4 tbsp of the wine and boil for 2 minutes, then simmer for a further 5 minutes. Add almost all the remaining wine and the lemon juice.

4 Place the salmon on top of the cooked mushrooms, cover with foil, and gently steam for 8–10 minutes, until just cooked. Remove the salmon from the pan and set aside.

5 Set aside the mushrooms and pour the cooking liquid into a large clean pan. Add the rice and cook for 10–15 minutes, until tender, adding more wine if necessary. Remove from the heat and stir in the dill and seasoning. Melt the remaining butter and fry the onion until brown. Set aside.

6 Grease a large baking tray. Flour a clean dish towel, place the pastry on it and roll into a rectangle 30 x 55cm/12 x 20in. Leaving 3cm/1¼in at the top and bottom ends of the pastry, place half the pancakes in a strip up the middle of the dough. Top with half the rice, half the onion, half the eggs and half the mushrooms. Place the salmon on top of the mushrooms and press down gently. Continue the layering process in reverse.

7 Take the 3cm/1¼in ends and wrap over the filling, then fold over the long edges. Brush with beaten egg and transfer to the baking sheet, rolling it so that it ends up seam side down. Chill for 1 hour. Cut 4 small slits in the top, brush with beaten egg and bake in a preheated oven at 220°C/425°F/Gas 7 for 10 minutes. Turn the oven down to 190°C/375°F/Gas 5 and cook for a further 30 minutes, until golden brown. Serve sliced, garnished with lemon and dill.

Creamy Creole Crab

INGREDIENTS

Serves 6

2 x 200g/7oz cans crab meat

3 hard-boiled eggs, shelled

5ml/1 tsp Dijon mustard

75g/3oz butter or margarine

1.5ml/¼ tsp cayenne pepper

45ml/3 tbsp sherry

30ml/2 tbsp chopped fresh parsley

120ml/4fl oz/½ cup single or
    whipping cream

2–3 thinly sliced spring onions, including
    some of the green parts

50g/2oz dried white breadcrumbs

salt and freshly ground black pepper

fresh chives and flat leaf parsley sprigs,
    to garnish

1 Flake the crab meat into a medium-sized bowl, keeping the pieces of crab as large as possible and removing any stray pieces of shell or cartilage.

2 In a medium-sized bowl, crumble the egg yolks with a fork. Add the mustard, 50g/2oz of the butter or margarine and the cayenne pepper, then mash together to form a paste. Mix in the sherry and parsley.

3 Chop the egg whites and mix in with the cream and spring onions. Stir in the crab meat and season well.

4 Divide the crab mixture equally among 6 greased scallop shells or individual baking dishes. Sprinkle with the breadcrumbs and dot with the remaining butter or margarine.

5 Bake in a preheated oven at 180°C/350°F/Gas 4 for about 20 minutes, until bubbling hot and golden brown. Serve, garnished with fresh chives and flat leaf parsley sprigs.

Crab with Spring Onions and Ginger

This recipe is far less complicated to make than it first appears. Buy live crabs, if you can, for the best flavour and texture.

Serves 4

1 large or 2 medium crabs, weighing about 675g/1½lb in total

30ml/2 tbsp Chinese rice wine or dry sherry

1 egg, lightly beaten

15ml/1 tbsp cornflour paste

45–60ml/3–4 tbsp vegetable oil

15ml/1 tbsp finely chopped fresh root ginger

3–4 spring onions, cut into short sections

30ml/2 tbsp light soy sauce

5ml/1 tsp soft light brown sugar

about 75ml/5 tbsp vegetable or chicken stock

few drops sesame oil

shredded spring onion, to garnish

stir-fried noodles, to serve

3 Heat the oil in a preheated wok and stir-fry the crab pieces, together with the chopped ginger and spring onions, for about 2–3 minutes.

4 Add the soy sauce, sugar and stock and blend well. Bring to the boil, cover and braise for 3–4 minutes. Sprinkle with sesame oil, garnish with spring onion and serve with stir-fried noodles.

1 Cut the crab in half from the underbelly. Break off the claws and crack them with the back of a cleaver. Discard the legs and crack the shell, breaking it into several pieces. Discard the feathery gills and the sac.

2 Put the crab pieces in a bowl. Mix together the rice wine or sherry, egg and cornflour paste, pour over the crab and set aside to marinate for 10–15 minutes.

Prawn Soufflé

This makes a very elegant lunch dish and is simple to prepare.

Serves 4–6

25g/1oz butter, plus extra for greasing

15ml/1 tbsp fine dried white breadcrumbs

175g/6oz cooked peeled prawns, deveined and coarsely chopped

15ml/1 tbsp finely chopped fresh tarragon or parsley

45ml/3 tbsp sherry or dry white wine

freshly ground black pepper

lemon slices, whole prawn and flat leaf parsley sprig, to garnish

For the soufflé mixture

40g/1½oz butter

37.5ml/2½ tbsp plain flour

250ml/8fl oz/1 cup milk, heated

4 eggs, separated, plus 1 egg white

salt

1 Butter a 1.5–1.75 litre/2½–3 pint/6¼–7½ cup soufflé dish. Sprinkle with the breadcrumbs, tilting the dish to coat the bottom and sides evenly.

2 Melt the butter in a small saucepan. Add the chopped prawns and cook for 2–3 minutes over a low heat. Stir in the tarragon or parsley and sherry or wine and season with pepper. Cook for a further 1–2 minutes. Raise the heat and boil rapidly to evaporate the liquid, then remove from the heat and set aside.

3 To make the soufflé mixture, melt the butter in a heavy-based saucepan. Add the flour, blending well with a wire whisk. Cook over a low heat for 2–3 minutes. Pour in the hot milk and whisk vigorously until smooth. Simmer for 2 minutes, still whisking, then season to taste with salt.

4 Remove the pan from the heat and immediately beat in the egg yolks, 1 at a time. Stir in the prawn mixture.

5 Whisk the egg whites in a large bowl until they form stiff peaks. Stir about one-quarter of the egg whites into the prawn mixture, then gently fold in the rest of the egg whites.

6 Carefully turn the mixture into the prepared dish. Bake in a preheated oven at 190°C/375°F/Gas 5 for about 30–40 minutes, until the soufflé is puffed up and light golden brown on top. Serve at once, with lemon slices, a whole prawn and a parsley sprig garnish.

VARIATIONS

For lobster soufflé, substitute 1 large lobster tail for the cooked prawns. Chop it finely and add to the saucepan with the herbs and wine in place of the prawns. For crab soufflé, instead of prawns, use about 175g/6oz fresh crab meat or a 200g/7oz can, drained. Flake and pick over carefully to remove any bits of shell.

Baked Mussels and Potatoes

This dish originates from Púglia in southern Italy, a region noted for its imaginative baked casseroles.

INGREDIENTS

Serves 2–3

675g/1½lb large mussels, in their shells

250ml/8fl oz/1 cup water

225g/8oz potatoes, unpeeled

75ml/5 tbsp olive oil

2 garlic cloves, finely chopped

8 fresh basil leaves, torn into pieces

225g/8oz tomatoes, skinned and
    thinly sliced

45ml/3 tbsp breadcrumbs

salt and freshly ground black pepper

1 Cut off the 'beards' from the mussels. Scrub and soak in several changes of cold water. Discard any with broken shells and ones that do not shut immediately when tapped sharply. Place the mussels with the water in a large saucepan over moderate heat. As soon as they open, lift them out. Remove and discard the empty half shells, leaving the mussels in the other half. (Discard any mussels that do not open.) Strain any liquid in the pan through a layer of kitchen paper and reserve.

2 Cook the potatoes in lightly salted boiling water until they are cooked, but still quite firm. Drain, peel and slice them.

3 Pour 30ml/2 tbsp of the olive oil into the base of a shallow ovenproof dish and tilt to coat. Cover with the potato slices in a single layer. Add the mussels in their half shells in a single layer. Sprinkle with chopped garlic and pieces of basil.

4 Cover with a layer of the tomato slices. Sprinkle with the breadcrumbs and black pepper, the reserved mussel cooking liquid and the remaining olive oil. Bake in a preheated oven at 180°C/350°F/Gas 4 for about 20 minutes, or until the tomatoes are soft and the breadcrumbs golden. Serve immediately.

Seafood in Puff Pastry

This classic combination of seafood in a creamy sauce served in a puff pastry case is found as an hors d'oeuvre on the menus of many elegant restaurants in France.

Serves 6

butter, for greasing

350g/12oz rough puff or puff pastry

1 egg beaten with 15ml/1 tbsp water, to glaze

60ml/4 tbsp dry white wine

2 shallots, finely chopped

450g/1lb mussels, scrubbed and 'debearded'

15g/½oz/1 tbsp butter

450g/1lb shelled scallops, cut in half crossways

450g/1lb raw prawns, peeled and deveined

175g/6oz cooked lobster meat, sliced

For the sauce

225g/8oz unsalted butter, diced

2 shallots, finely chopped

250ml/8fl oz/1 cup fish stock

90ml/6 tbsp dry white wine

15–30ml/1–2 tbsp double cream

lemon juice

salt and freshly ground white pepper

fresh dill sprigs, to garnish

1 Lightly grease a large baking sheet and sprinkle with a little water. On a lightly floured surface, roll out the pastry into a rectangle slightly less than 5mm/¼in thick. Using a sharp knife, cut into 6 diamond shapes about 13cm/5in long. Transfer to the baking sheet. Brush the pastry with the egg glaze. Using the tip of a knife, score a line 1cm/½in from the edge, then lightly mark the centre in a criss-cross pattern.

2 Chill the pastry cases for 30 minutes. Bake in a preheated oven at 220°C/425°F/Gas 7 for about 20 minutes, until puffed and brown. Transfer to a wire rack and, while still hot, remove each lid, cutting along the scored line to free it. Scoop out any uncooked dough from the bases and discard, then leave the cases to cool completely.

3 In a large saucepan, bring the wine and shallots to the boil over a high heat. Add the mussels to the pan, cover tightly and cook, shaking the pan occasionally, for 4–6 minutes, until the shells open. Remove any mussels that do not open. Reserve 6 mussels for the garnish, then remove the rest from their shells and set aside in a bowl, covered. Strain the cooking liquid through a muslin-lined sieve and reserve for the sauce.

4 In a heavy frying pan, melt the butter over a medium heat. Add the scallops and prawns, cover tightly and cook for 3–4 minutes, shaking and stirring occasionally, until they feel just firm to the touch; do not overcook.

5 Using a slotted spoon, transfer the scallops and prawns to the bowl with the mussels and add any cooking juices to the reserved mussel cooking liquid.

6 To make the sauce, melt 25g/1oz of the butter in a heavy saucepan. Add the shallots and cook for 2 minutes. Pour in the fish stock and boil for about 15 minutes over a high heat, until reduced by three-quarters. Add the white wine and reserved cooking liquid and boil for 5–7 minutes, until reduced by half. Lower the heat to medium and whisk in the remaining butter, a little at a time, to make a smooth thick sauce (lift the pan from the heat if the sauce begins to boil). Whisk in the cream and season with salt, if needed, pepper and lemon juice. Keep the sauce warm over a very low heat, stirring frequently.

7 Warm the pastry cases in a low oven for about 10 minutes. Put the mussels, scallops and prawns in a large saucepan. Stir in a quarter of the sauce and reheat gently over a low heat. Gently stir in the lobster meat and cook for 1 further minute.

8 Arrange the pastry case bases on individual plates. Divide the seafood mixture equally among them and top with the lids. Garnish each with a mussel in its half-shell and a dill sprig and spoon the remaining sauce around the edges or serve separately.

Puff Pastry Salmon with Chanterelle Cream

The slightly bland flavour of farmed salmon is helped by a creamy layer of chanterelle mushrooms.

INGREDIENTS

Serves 6

675g/1½lb puff pastry, thawed
    if frozen
1 egg, beaten, to glaze
2 large salmon fillets, about 900g/2lb total
    weight, skinned and boned
375ml/13fl oz/1⅝ cups dry white wine
1 small carrot
1 small onion, halved
½ celery stick, chopped
1 thyme sprig
kale, to garnish

For the chanterelle cream
25g/1oz unsalted butter
2 shallots, chopped
225g/8oz chanterelle mushrooms,
    trimmed and sliced
75ml/5 tbsp white wine
150ml/¼ pint/⅔ cup double cream
45ml/3 tbsp chopped fresh chervil
30ml/2 tbsp chopped fresh chives

For the hollandaise sauce
175g/6oz unsalted butter
2 egg yolks
10ml/2 tsp lemon juice
salt and freshly ground black pepper

1 Roll out the pastry on a floured surface to form a rectangle 10cm/4in longer and 5cm/2in wider than the fillets. Trim into a fish shape, decorate with a pastry cutter to represent scales and glaze with beaten egg. Chill for 1 hour and then bake in a preheated oven at 200°C/400°F/Gas 6 for about 30–35 minutes, until well risen and golden. Remove from the oven and split open horizontally. Reduce the oven temperature to 170°C/325°F/Gas 3.

2 To make the chanterelle cream, melt the butter and fry the shallots gently until soft but not coloured. Add the mushrooms and cook until their juices begin to run. Pour in the wine, increase the heat and boil to evaporate the liquid. When dry, add the cream and herbs and bring to a simmer. Season well, transfer to a bowl, cover and keep warm.

3 Place the salmon in a fish kettle or roasting tin. Add the wine, carrot, onion, celery, thyme and enough water to cover. Slowly bring just to boiling point, remove from the heat, cover and allow the fish to cook in this gentle heat for 30 minutes.

4 To make the sauce, melt the butter, skim the surface and pour into a jug, leaving behind the milky residue. Place the egg yolks and 15ml/1 tbsp of water in a glass bowl and place over a pan of simmering water. Whisk the yolks until thick and foamy. Remove from the heat and very slowly pour in the butter, whisking all the time. Add the lemon juice and season.

5 Place one salmon fillet on the base of the pastry, spread with the chanterelle cream and cover with the second fillet. Cover with the top of the pastry 'fish' and warm through in the oven for about 10–15 minutes. Garnish with kale and serve with the sauce.

Whole Cooked Salmon

Farmed salmon has made this fish more affordable and less of a treat, but a whole salmon still features as a centrepiece at parties. It is never served with cold meats, but is usually accompanied by salads and mayonnaise. As with all fish, the taste depends on freshness and on not overcooking it, so although you need to start the preparation early, the cooking time is short.

INGREDIENTS

Serves about 10 as part of a buffet

2–3kg/5–6lb fresh whole salmon

30ml/2 tbsp oil

1 lemon

salt and freshly ground black pepper

lemon wedges, cucumber and fresh dill
    sprigs, to garnish

1 Wash the salmon and dry it well, inside and out. Pour half the oil on to a large piece of strong foil and place the fish in the centre.

2 Put a few slices of lemon inside the salmon and arrange some more on the top. Season well and sprinkle over the remaining oil. Wrap up the foil to make a loose parcel. Put the parcel on another sheet of foil or a baking sheet and cook in a preheated oven at 200°C/400°F/Gas 6 for 10 minutes. Turn off the oven, do not open the door and leave for several hours.

3 To serve the same day, remove the foil and peel off the skin. If you are keeping it for the following day, leave the skin on and chill the fish overnight. Arrange the fish on a large platter and garnish with lemon wedges, cucumber cut into thin ribbons and sprigs of dill.

Baked Stuffed Sardines

Serve this nutritious dish with a fresh tomato salad and fresh bread.

Serves 4

12 fresh sardines, gutted, scaled and
    heads removed
15ml/1 tbsp sunflower oil, plus extra for
    greasing
1 onion, finely chopped
1 garlic clove, crushed
75g/3oz fresh wholemeal breadcrumbs
15ml/1 tbsp wholegrain mustard
30ml/2 tbsp chopped fresh parsley
1 egg yolk
30ml/2 tbsp grated Parmesan cheese
grated rind and juice of 2 lemons
salt and freshly ground black pepper
lemon wedges and flat leaf parsley,
    to garnish

1 Using a sharp knife, slit the sardines open along their undersides, then turn each fish over and press it firmly along the back to loosen the backbone. Carefully remove the backbones and clean and dry the inside of each sardine thoroughly.

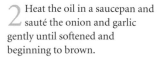

2 Heat the oil in a saucepan and sauté the onion and garlic gently until softened and beginning to brown.

3 Remove the pan from the heat and mix in the breadcrumbs, mustard, chopped parsley, egg yolk and Parmesan cheese. Stir in half the lemon rind and juice and season to taste.

4 Use the stuffing to fill the cavities of the sardines.

5 Brush a shallow ovenproof dish lightly with oil and add the sardines, in a single layer. Add the remaining lemon rind and juice, cover with foil and bake in a preheated oven at 190°C/375°F/ Gas 5 for 30 minutes. Garnish with the lemon wedges and fresh parsley sprigs.

COOK'S TIP

Oily fish are a good source of vitamins A and D and are low in saturated fat. Larger oily fish, such as mackerel or herring, could be substituted for the sardines in this recipe. Allow one fish per person.

Mediterranean Baked Fish

This informal fish bake is said to have originated with the fishermen on the Cote d'Azur, who would cook the remains of their catch for lunch in the still-warm baker's oven.

INGREDIENTS

Serves 4

3 medium potatoes

30ml/2 tbsp olive oil, plus extra for drizzling

2 onions, halved and sliced

2 garlic cloves, very finely chopped

675g/1½lb thick, skinless fish fillets, such as turbot or sea bass

1 bay leaf

1 thyme sprig

3 tomatoes, skinned and thinly sliced

30ml/2 tbsp orange juice

60ml/4 tbsp dry white wine

2.5ml/½ tsp saffron threads, steeped in 60ml/4 tbsp boiling water

salt and freshly ground black pepper

1 Cook the potatoes in boiling salted water for 15 minutes, then drain. When the potatoes are cool enough to handle, peel off the skins and slice them thinly.

COOK'S TIP

Both turbot and sea bass have a very delicate flavour, which can easily be destroyed by too rich a sauce or by overcooking.

2 Meanwhile, heat the oil in a heavy frying pan and fry the onions over a medium-low heat for about 10 minutes, stirring frequently. Add the garlic and continue cooking for a few minutes more, until the onions are soft and golden.

3 Layer half the potato slices in a 2 litre/3⅓ pint/8 cup baking dish. Cover with half the onions. Season with salt and pepper.

4 Place the fish fillets on top of the vegetables and tuck in the herbs between them. Top with the tomato slices and then the remaining onions and potatoes.

5 Pour over the orange juice, wine and saffron liquid, season with salt and pepper and drizzle a little extra olive oil on top. Bake in a preheated oven at 190°C/375°F/Gas 5, uncovered, for about 30 minutes, until the potatoes are tender and the fish is cooked.

Baked Cod with Garlic Mayonnaise

This unusual way of preparing cod is adapted from an Italian recipe for more typical Mediterranean fish.

Serves 4

4 anchovy fillets
45ml/3 tbsp chopped fresh parsley
90ml/6 tbsp olive oil
4 cod fillets, about 675g/1½lb
    total, skinned
40g/1½oz plain breadcrumbs
coarsely ground black pepper

For the garlic mayonnaise
2 garlic cloves, finely chopped
1 egg yolk
5ml/1 tsp Dijon mustard
175ml/6fl oz/¾ cup vegetable oil
salt and freshly ground black pepper

1 Make the mayonnaise. First put the garlic in a mortar or small bowl and mash it to a paste. Beat in the egg yolk and mustard. Add the oil in a continuous thin stream, while beating vigorously with a small wire whisk. When the mixture is thick and smooth, season with salt and pepper. Cover the bowl and keep cool.

2 Chop the anchovy fillets with the parsley very finely. Place in a small bowl and add pepper to taste and 45ml/3 tbsp of the oil. Stir to a paste.

3 Place the cod fillets in a single layer in an oiled baking dish. Spread the anchovy paste on the top of the cod fillets. Sprinkle with the breadcrumbs and the remaining oil. Bake in a preheated oven at 200°C/400°F/Gas 6 for 20–25 minutes, or until the bread-crumbs are golden. Serve hot with the garlic mayonnaise.

Monkfish Medallions with Thyme

Monkfish has a sweet flesh that combines particularly well with Mediterranean flavours.

Serves 4

500g/1¼lb monkfish fillet, preferably in a
    single piece
45ml/3 tbsp extra virgin olive oil
75g/3oz small black olives, stoned
1 large or 2 small tomatoes, seeded
    and diced
1 fresh thyme sprig or 5ml/1 tsp dried
    thyme leaves
salt and freshly ground black pepper
15ml/1 tbsp very finely chopped fresh
    parsley, to garnish

1 Remove the grey membrane from the monkfish, if necessary. Cut the fish into slices 1cm/½in thick.

2 Heat a non-stick frying pan until it is quite hot, without oil. Sear the fish quickly on both sides. Remove and set aside.

3 Pour 15ml/1 tbsp of the olive oil in the base of a shallow baking dish and tilt to coat. Arrange the fish in a single layer. Scatter the olives and diced tomato on top of the fish.

4 Sprinkle the fish with thyme, salt and pepper and the remaining oil. Bake in a preheated oven at 200°C/400°F/Gas 6 for 10–12 minutes.

5 To serve, divide the medallions between 4 warmed plates. Spoon on the vegetables and any cooking juices. Sprinkle with the chopped parsley.

Stuffed Plaice Rolls

Plaice fillets are an excellent choice for family meals because they are economical, easy to cook and free of bones – besides being delicious.

Serves 4

2 medium carrots, grated

1 medium courgette, grated

60ml/4 tbsp fresh wholemeal
    breadcrumbs

15ml/1 tbsp lime or lemon juice

4 plaice fillets

salt and freshly ground black pepper

boiled new potatoes, to serve

1 Mix together the grated carrots and courgette. Stir in the breadcrumbs and lime juice and season with salt and pepper.

2 Lay the fish fillets skin side up and divide the stuffing between them, spreading it evenly.

3 Roll up to enclose the stuffing and place in an ovenproof dish. Cover and bake in a preheated oven at 200°C/400°F/Gas 6 for about 30 minutes, or until the fish flakes easily. Serve hot with new potatoes.

COOK'S TIP

If you like, you can remove the skin from the plaice fillets before cooking. This recipe creates its own delicious juices, but for an extra sauce, stir chopped fresh parsley into a little fromage frais and serve with the fish.

Fillets of Hake Baked with Thyme

Quick cooking is the essence of this dish. Use the freshest garlic available and, if there is no fresh thyme, use half the amount of dried thyme.

Serves 4

4 x 175g/6oz hake fillets

1 shallot, finely chopped

2 garlic cloves, thinly sliced

4 fresh thyme sprigs

grated rind and juice of 1 lemon, plus
    extra juice for drizzling

30ml/2 tbsp extra virgin olive oil

salt and freshly ground black pepper

finely grated lemon rind and fresh thyme
    sprigs, to garnish

2 Season well with salt and freshly ground pepper.

3 Drizzle over the lemon juice and olive oil. Bake in a preheated oven at 180°C/350°F/Gas 4 for about 15 minutes, or until the fish flakes easily. Serve, garnished with finely grated lemon rind and fresh thyme sprigs.

VARIATIONS

If hake is not available, you can use cod or haddock fillets for this recipe. You can also use a mixture of fresh herbs, such as tarragon, parsley and chervil.

1 Arrange the hake fillets on the base of a large roasting tin. Scatter the shallot, garlic cloves and thyme on top.

COOK'S TIP
~

Hake is a round fish extensively found in the North and South Atlantic and is extremely popular in Spain and Portugal. Its milky white flesh is delicate in flavour and quite fragile, so fillets need very careful handling, as they break up easily.

Breaded Fish with Tartare Sauce

All the taste of the classic British fish dish but without any frying.

Serves 4

50g/2oz dried breadcrumbs
5ml/1 tsp dried oregano
2.5ml/½ tsp cayenne pepper
250ml/8fl oz/1 cup milk
10ml/2 tsp salt
4 pieces of cod fillet, about 675g/1½lb
40g/1½oz butter or margarine, melted

For the tartare sauce

120ml/4fl oz/½ cup mayonnaise
2.5ml/½ tsp Dijon mustard
1–2 pickled gherkins, finely chopped
15ml/1 tbsp drained capers, chopped
5ml/1 tsp chopped fresh parsley
5ml/1 tsp chopped fresh chives
5ml/1 tsp chopped fresh tarragon
salt and freshly ground black pepper

1 Grease a shallow ovenproof baking dish. Combine the breadcrumbs, oregano and cayenne pepper on a plate and blend together. Mix the milk with the salt in a bowl, stirring well to dissolve the salt.

2 Dip the pieces of cod fillet in the milk, then transfer to the plate and coat with the bread-crumb mixture.

3 Arrange the coated fish in the prepared baking dish, in a single layer. Drizzle the melted butter or margarine over the fish.

4 Bake in a preheated oven at 230°C/450°F/Gas 8 for about 10–15 minutes, until the fish flakes easily when tested with a fork.

5 Meanwhile, combine all the ingredients for the tartare sauce in a small bowl. Stir gently to mix thoroughly. Serve the fish hot, accompanied by the tartare sauce, handed separately.

Smoked Haddock Lyonnaise

Lyonnaise dishes take their name from the city of Lyons, known for its excellent food. The term 'Lyonnaise' refers to dishes prepared or garnished with onions.

INGREDIENTS

Serves 4

450g/1lb smoked haddock
150ml/¼ pint/⅔ cup milk
15g/½oz butter
2 onions, chopped
15ml/1 tbsp cornflour
150ml/¼ pint/⅔ cup Greek-style yogurt
5ml/1 tsp ground turmeric
5ml/1 tsp paprika
115g/4oz mushrooms, sliced
2 celery sticks, chopped
30ml/2 tbsp olive oil
350g/12oz firm cooked potatoes,
    preferably cold, diced
25–50g/1–2oz soft white breadcrumbs
salt and freshly ground black pepper
flat leaf parsley, to garnish

2 Melt the butter and fry half the chopped onions until translucent. Stir in the cornflour, then gradually blend in the fish cooking liquid and the yogurt and cook until thickened and smooth.

3 Stir in the turmeric, paprika, mushrooms and celery. Season to taste and add the flaked fish. Spoon into an ovenproof dish.

4 Heat the oil and fry the remaining onions until translucent. Add the diced potatoes and stir until lightly coated in oil. Sprinkle on the breadcrumbs and seasoning.

5 Spoon this mixture over the fish and bake in a preheated oven at 190°C/375°F/Gas 5 for 20–30 minutes.

1 Put the smoked haddock and the milk into a large pan over a low heat and poach the fish for about 15 minutes, until just cooked. Remove the haddock, reserving the cooking liquid, then flake the fish and discard the skin and any bones. Set aside.

Sand Dab Provençal

Recreate the taste of the Mediterranean with this easy-to-make fish bake.

Serves 4

4 large sand dab fillets
2 small red onions
120ml/4fl oz/½ cup vegetable stock
60ml/4 tbsp dry red wine
1 garlic clove, crushed
2 courgettes, sliced
1 yellow pepper, seeded and sliced
400g/14oz can chopped tomatoes
15ml/1 tbsp chopped fresh thyme
salt and freshly ground black pepper
potato gratin, to serve (optional)

1 Skin the sand dab fillets with a sharp knife by laying them skin side down. Holding the tail end, push the knife between the skin and flesh in a sawing movement. Hold the knife at an angle with the blade angled towards the skin.

2 Cut each onion into 8 wedges. Put into a heavy-based saucepan, together with the stock. Cover and simmer for 5 minutes. Uncover and continue to cook, stirring occasionally, until the stock has reduced entirely. Add the wine and garlic clove to the pan and continue to cook until the onions are soft.

3 Add the courgettes, yellow pepper, tomatoes and thyme and season with salt and pepper to taste. Simmer for 3 minutes. Spoon the sauce into a large casserole.

4 Fold each fillet in half and place on top of the sauce. Cover and cook in a preheated oven at 180°C/350°F/Gas 4 for 15–20 minutes, until the fish is opaque and cooked. Serve at once with potato gratin, if liked.

Stuffed Swordfish Rolls

Swordfish is abundant around Sicily and it features in many dishes there.

Serves 4

4 slices fresh swordfish about 1cm/
    ½ in thick
90ml/6 tbsp olive oil
1 garlic clove, finely chopped (optional)
50g/2oz breadcrumbs
30ml/2 tbsp capers, rinsed, drained
    and chopped
10 leaves fresh basil, chopped
60ml/4 tbsp fresh lemon juice
salt and freshly ground black pepper

For the tomato sauce
30ml/2 tbsp olive oil
1 garlic clove, crushed
1 small onion, finely chopped
450g/1lb tomatoes, skinned
120ml/4fl oz/½ cup dry white wine
salt and freshly ground black pepper

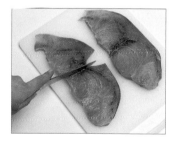

1 Cut the swordfish slices in half, removing any bones. Brush with 30ml/2 tbsp of the olive oil, and refrigerate until needed.

2 Make the tomato sauce by heating the oil in a medium-sized heavy saucepan. Add the garlic, and cook until golden. Discard the garlic. Add the onion, and cook over a low heat until soft. Stir in the tomatoes and wine. Season with salt and pepper. Cover the pan, and cook over moderate heat for 15 minutes.

3 Pass the sauce through a food mill or purée in a food processor. Keep warm while you prepare the fish.

4 In a small bowl combine 30ml/2 tbsp of olive oil with the garlic, if using, breadcrumbs, capers, basil and lemon juice. Season with salt and pepper and mix to a paste.

5 Lay the swordfish slices flat on a chopping board. Divide the stuffing mixture equally between the slices and spread it evenly over the centre of each. Roll up the swordfish slices and secure with wooden cocktail sticks.

6 Heat the remaining oil in a flameproof dish. Add the swordfish rolls and brown them for 3–4 minutes over a high heat, turning them once or twice. Pour in the tomato sauce and bake in a preheated oven at 200°C/400°F/ Gas 6 for 15 minutes, basting from time to time. Serve warm.

Halibut with Fennel and Orange

The lovely sweet flavour of halibut can take strong accents like fennel and orange.

Serves 4

50g/2oz butter, plus extra for greasing
1 fennel bulb, thinly sliced
grated rind and juice of 1 orange
150ml/¼ pint/⅔ cup dry white wine
4 halibut steaks, about 200g/7oz each
salt and freshly ground black pepper
fresh fennel fronds, to garnish

1 Butter a shallow baking dish and set aside. Add the fennel to a saucepan of boiling water, return to the boil and cook for about 4–6 minutes, until just tender.

2 Meanwhile, put the orange rind, juice and wine in a small pan and boil until reduced by half.

3 Drain the fennel, then arrange in the baking dish and season. Arrange the halibut on the fennel, season, dot with butter, then pour over the reduced orange and wine.

4 Cover and bake in a preheated oven at 180°C/350°F/Gas 4 for about 20 minutes, until the flesh flakes. Serve immediately, garnished with fennel fronds.

Salmon with Cucumber Sauce

Cucumber and fresh dill are a perfect combination in this unusual hot sauce, which really complements the baked salmon.

Serves 6–8

1.8kg/4lb salmon, gutted and scaled
melted butter, for brushing
3 parsley or thyme sprigs
½ lemon, halved
fresh dill sprigs, to garnish
orange slices and salad leaves, to serve

For the cucumber sauce
1 large cucumber, peeled
25g/1oz butter
120ml/4fl oz/½ cup dry white wine
45ml/3 tbsp finely chopped fresh dill
60ml/4 tbsp soured cream
salt and freshly ground black pepper

1 Season the salmon and brush inside and out with melted butter. Place the herb sprigs and lemon in the cavity.

2 Wrap the salmon in foil, folding the edges together securely, then bake in a preheated oven at 220°C/425°F/Gas 7 for 15 minutes. Remove the fish from the oven and leave in the foil for 1 hour, then remove the skin from the salmon.

3 Meanwhile, halve the cucumber lengthways, scoop out the seeds, then dice the flesh.

4 Place the cucumber in a colander, toss lightly with salt and leave for about 30 minutes to drain. Rinse well and pat dry.

5 Heat the butter in a small saucepan, add the cucumber and cook for about 2 minutes, until translucent but not soft. Add the wine to the pan and boil briskly until the cucumber is dry.

6 Stir the dill and soured cream into the cucumber and season to taste. Fillet the salmon and garnish with the fresh dill. Serve immediately with the cucumber sauce, orange slices and salad.

Sea Bass with Citrus Fruit

The sea bass family is found throughout most of the world's seas and is especially popular along the Mediterranean coast. Its delicate flavour is complemented by citrus fruits and fruity French olive oil.

INGREDIENTS

Serves 6

1 small grapefruit

1 orange

1 lemon

1 sea bass, about 1.35kg/3lb, cleaned
    and scaled

6 fresh basil sprigs

6 fresh dill sprigs

plain flour, for dusting

45ml/3 tbsp olive oil

4–6 shallots, halved

60ml/4 tbsp dry white wine

15g/½oz butter

salt and freshly ground black pepper

1 Using a vegetable peeler, remove the rind from the grapefruit, orange and lemon. Cut into thin julienne strips, cover and set aside. Peel off the white pith from the fruits and, working over a bowl to catch the juices, cut out the segments from the grapefruit and orange and set aside for the garnish. Slice the lemon thickly.

2 Wipe the fish dry inside and out and season the cavity with salt and pepper. Make 3 diagonal slashes on each side. Reserve a few basil and dill sprigs for the garnish and fill the cavity with the remaining basil, dill, the lemon slices and half the julienne strips of citrus rind.

3 Dust the fish lightly with flour. In a roasting tin or flameproof casserole large enough to hold the fish, heat 30ml/2 tbsp of the olive oil over a medium-high heat and cook the fish for about 1 minute, until the skin just crisps and browns on one side. Add the halved shallots.

4 Bake the fish in a preheated oven at190°C/375°F/Gas 5 for about 15 minutes, then carefully turn the fish over and stir the shallots. Drizzle the fish with the remaining oil and bake for a further 10–15 minutes, until the flesh is opaque throughout.

5 Carefully transfer the fish to a heated serving dish and remove and discard the cavity stuffing. Pour off any excess oil and add the wine and 30–45ml/ 2–3 tbsp of the fruit juices to the pan. Bring to the boil over a high heat, stirring. Stir in the remaining julienne strips of citrus rind and boil for 2–3 minutes, then whisk in the butter. Spoon the shallots and sauce around the fish and garnish with dill and the reserved basil and grapefruit and orange segments.

Sesame Baked Fish

Tropical fish are found increasingly in supermarkets, but Asian markets usually have a wider selection.

INGREDIENTS

Serves 4–6

2 red snapper, parrot fish, or monkfish
    tails, weighing about 350g/12oz each
30ml/2 tbsp vegetable oil
10ml/2 tsp sesame oil
30ml/2 tbsp sesame seeds
2.5cm/1 in piece fresh root ginger,
    thinly sliced
2 garlic cloves, crushed
2 small fresh red chillies, seeded and
    finely chopped
4 shallots or 1 medium onion, halved
    and sliced
30ml/2 tbsp water
1cm/½in square piece shrimp paste or
    15ml/1 tbsp fish sauce
10ml/2 tsp caster sugar
2.5ml/½ tsp cracked black pepper
juice of 2 limes
3–4 banana leaves or aluminium foil
lime wedges, to garnish (optional)

2 To make the marinade, heat the vegetable and sesame oils in a preheated wok, add the sesame seeds and fry until golden. Add the ginger, garlic, chillies and shallots or onion and soften over a gentle heat without burning. Add the water, shrimp paste or fish sauce, sugar, pepper, and lime juice. Simmer for 2–3 minutes and set aside to cool.

3 If using banana leaves, remove and discard the central stem. Soften the leaves by dipping them in boiling water. To keep them supple, rub all over with vegetable oil. Spread the marinade over the fish, wrap in the banana leaves, and fasten with bamboo skewers, or wrap the fish in aluminium foil. Leave in a cool place for up to 3 hours to allow the flavours to mingle.

4 Place the wrapped fish on a baking sheet and bake in a preheated oven at 180°C/350°F/Gas 4 for 35–40 minutes. Alternatively, place on a wire rack and cook over a barbecue for 35–40 minutes. Garnish with lime wedges, if liked, and serve hot.

1 Clean the fish inside and out under cold running water. Pat dry with kitchen paper. Score both sides of each fish deeply with a knife to enable the marinade to penetrate effectively. If using parrot fish, rub with fine salt and leave to stand for 15 minutes. (This will remove the chalky coral flavour often associated with the parrot fish.)

Tahini Baked Fish

This dish is a favourite in many Middle Eastern countries, especially Egypt, Lebanon and Syria.

INGREDIENTS

Serves 6

6 cod or haddock fillets
juice of 2 lemons
60ml/4 tbsp olive oil
2 large onions, chopped
250ml/8fl oz/1 cup tahini
1 garlic clove, crushed
45–60ml/3–4 tbsp water
salt and freshly ground black pepper
rice and salad, to serve

1 Arrange the cod or haddock fillets in a large shallow casserole or baking dish, pour over 15ml/1 tbsp of the lemon juice and 15ml/1 tbsp of the olive oil and bake in a preheated oven at 180°C/350°F/ Gas 4 for about 20 minutes.

2 Meanwhile, heat the remaining oil in a large frying pan and fry the onions for 6–8 minutes, until well browned and almost crisp.

3 Put the tahini and garlic in a small bowl and gradually beat in the remaining lemon juice and water, a little at a time, until the sauce is light and creamy. Season to taste with salt and pepper.

4 Sprinkle the onions over the fish and pour over the tahini sauce. Bake the fish for a further 15 minutes, until the flesh is cooked through and the sauce is bubbling. Serve the fish at once with rice and a salad.

Roast Monkfish with Garlic and Fennel

Monkfish was sometimes used as a substitute for lobster meat because it is very similar in texture. It is now appreciated in its own right and is delicious quickly roasted.

INGREDIENTS

Serves 4

1.1kg/2½lb monkfish tail
8 garlic cloves
15ml/1 tbsp olive oil
2 bulbs fennel, sliced
juice of 1 lemon
1 bay leaf
salt and freshly ground black pepper
fresh bay leaves and finely grated lemon
    rind, to garnish

4 Peel and finely slice the garlic cloves and cut incisions into the fish flesh. Place the garlic slices into the incisions.

5 Heat the oil in a large, heavy-based saucepan and seal the fish on all sides.

6 Place the fish in a roasting tin, together with the fennel, lemon juice, seasoning and bay leaf. Roast in a preheated oven at 220°C/425°F/Gas 7 for about 20 minutes, until cooked through. Garnish with bay leaves and lemon rind and serve immediately.

1 With a filleting knife, cut away the thin, transparent membrane covering the outside of the fish to avoid its shrinking.

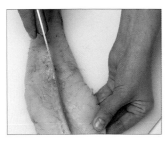

2 Cut along 1 side of the central bone to remove the fillet. Repeat on the other side.

3 Tie the fillets together with string.

CASSEROLES
AND STEWS

Green Curry of Prawns

A popular, fragrant, creamy curry that also takes very little time to prepare. It can also be made with thin strips of chicken meat.

INGREDIENTS

Serves 4–6

30ml/2 tbsp vegetable oil

30ml/2 tbsp green curry paste

450g/1lb raw king prawns, peeled and deveined

4 kaffir lime leaves, torn

1 lemon grass stalk, bruised and chopped

250ml/8fl oz/1 cup coconut milk

30ml/2 tbsp fish sauce

½ cucumber, seeded and cut into thin batons

10–15 basil leaves

4 green chillies, sliced, to garnish

1 Heat the oil in a frying pan. Add the green curry paste and fry until bubbling and fragrant.

2 Add the prawns, kaffir lime leaves and lemon grass. Fry for 1–2 minutes, until the prawns have just turned pink.

3 Stir in the coconut milk and bring to a gentle boil. Simmer, stirring occasionally, for about 5 minutes, or until the prawns are tender. Do not overcook them.

4 Stir in the fish sauce, cucumber and basil, then top with the green chillies and serve.

Green Fish Curry

This dish combines all the typical flavours of the East.

Serves 4

1.5ml/¼ tsp ground turmeric

30ml/2 tbsp lime juice

4 cod fillets, skinned and cut into
    5cm/2in chunks

1 onion, chopped

1 fresh large green chilli, roughly
    chopped

1 garlic clove, crushed

25g/1oz cashew nuts

2.5ml/½ tsp fennel seeds

30ml/2 tbsp desiccated coconut

30ml/2 tbsp oil

1.5ml/¼ tsp cumin seeds

1.5ml/¼ tsp ground coriander

1.5ml/¼ tsp ground cumin

150ml/¼ pint/⅔ cup water

175ml/6fl oz/¾ cup single cream

45ml/3 tbsp finely chopped
    fresh coriander

salt

fresh coriander sprig, to garnish

vegetable pilau, to serve (optional)

1 Mix together the turmeric, lime juice and a pinch of salt and rub over the fish. Cover and leave to marinate for 15 minutes.

2 Meanwhile work the onion, chilli, garlic, cashew nuts, fennel seeds and coconut to a paste in a food processor or in a mortar with a pestle. Spoon the paste into a bowl and set aside.

3 Heat the oil in a large frying pan and fry the cumin seeds for 2 minutes, until they begin to splutter. Add the spice paste and fry for 5 minutes, then stir in the ground coriander, cumin and water. Fry, stirring frequently, for about 2–3 minutes.

4 Add the single cream and the fresh coriander. Simmer for 5 minutes. Add the fish and gently stir in. Cover and cook gently for 10 minutes, until the fish is tender. Garnish with a coriander sprig and serve with vegetable pilau, if liked.

Prawn Curry with Quails' Eggs

Quails' eggs are available from speciality shops and delicatessens. Hens' eggs may be substituted if quails' eggs are hard to find. Use 1 hen's egg to every 4 quails' eggs.

INGREDIENTS

Serves 4

12 quails' eggs

30ml/2 tbsp vegetable oil

4 shallots or 1 medium onion,
    finely chopped

2.5cm/1in piece galingal or fresh root
    ginger, chopped

2 garlic cloves, crushed

5cm/2in piece lemon grass,
    finely shredded

1–2 small, fresh red chillies, seeded and
    finely chopped

2.5ml/½ tsp turmeric

1cm/½ in square piece shrimp paste or
    15ml/1 tbsp fish sauce

900g/2lb raw prawn tails, peeled
    and deveined

400ml/14fl oz/1⅔ cups canned
    coconut milk

300ml/½ pint/1¼ cups chicken stock

115g/4oz Chinese leaves,
    roughly shredded

10ml/2 tsp sugar

2.5ml/½ tsp salt

2 spring onions, green part only,
    shredded, and 30ml/2 tbsp shredded
    coconut, to garnish

1 Cook the quails' eggs in boiling water for 8 minutes. Refresh in cold water, peel and then set aside.

2 Heat the vegetable oil in a large wok, add the shallots or onion, galingal or ginger and garlic and soften without colouring. Add the lemon grass, chillies, turmeric and shrimp paste or fish sauce and fry briefly to bring out their flavours.

3 Add the prawns and fry briefly. Pour the coconut milk through a strainer over a bowl, then add the thin part of the milk with the chicken stock. Add the Chinese leaves, sugar and salt and bring to the boil. Simmer for 6–8 minutes.

4 Turn out on to a serving dish, halve the quails' eggs and toss in the sauce. Scatter with the spring onions and the shredded coconut and serve.

Parsi Prawn Curry

This dish comes from the west coast of India, where fresh seafood is eaten in abundance. Fresh king prawns or tiger prawns are ideal.

INGREDIENTS

Serves 4–6

60ml/4 tbsp vegetable oil
3 medium onions, 1 finely sliced and
    2 finely chopped
6 garlic cloves, finely crushed
5ml/1 tsp chilli powder
7.5ml/1½ tsp turmeric
50ml/2fl oz/¼ cup tamarind juice
5ml/1 tsp mint sauce
15ml/1 tbsp demerara sugar
450g/1lb raw king prawns, peeled
    and deveined
75g/3oz coriander leaves, chopped
salt
fresh coriander sprig, to garnish

1 Heat the oil in a frying pan and fry the sliced onion until golden brown. In a bowl, mix the garlic, chilli powder and turmeric with a little water to form a paste. Add to the browned onion and simmer for 3 minutes.

2 Add the chopped onions and fry until they become translucent, then fold in the tamarind juice, mint sauce, sugar and salt. Simmer for a further 3 minutes.

3 Pat the prawns dry with kitchen paper. Add to the spice mixture with a small amount of water and stir-fry until the prawns turn a bright orange-pink colour.

4 When the prawns are cooked, add the chopped coriander leaves and stir-fry over a high heat for a few minutes to thicken the sauce. Garnish with the coriander and serve hot.

Pineapple Curry with Prawns and Mussels

The delicate sweet and sour flavour of this curry comes from the pineapple and although it seems an odd combination, it is absolutely delicious. Use the freshest shellfish that you can find.

INGREDIENTS

Serves 4–6

600ml/1 pint/2½ cups coconut milk
30ml/2 tbsp red curry paste
30ml/2 tbsp fish sauce
15ml/1 tbsp granulated sugar
225g/8oz raw king prawns, shelled and
    deveined
450g/1lb mussels, cleaned and
    'beards' removed
175g/6oz fresh pineapple, finely crushed
    or chopped
5 kaffir lime leaves, torn
2 red chillies, chopped and coriander
    leaves, to garnish

1 Bring half the coconut milk to the boil and heat, stirring, until it separates.

2 Add the red curry paste and cook until fragrant. Add the fish sauce and sugar and continue to cook for a few moments.

3 Stir in the rest of the coconut milk and bring back to the boil. Add the king prawns, mussels, pineapple and kaffir lime leaves.

4 Reheat until boiling and then simmer for 3–5 minutes, until the prawns are cooked and the mussels have opened. Remove any mussels that have not opened and discard. Serve immediately, garnished with chopped red chillies and coriander leaves.

Curried Prawns in Coconut Milk

A curry-like dish where the prawns are cooked in a spicy coconut gravy.

INGREDIENTS

Serves 4–6

600ml/1 pint/2½ cups coconut milk
30ml/2 tbsp yellow curry paste
15ml/1 tbsp fish sauce
2.5ml/½ tsp salt
5ml/1 tsp granulated sugar
450g/1lb raw king prawns, shelled and
    deveined
225g/8oz cherry tomatoes
juice of ½ lime, to serve
red chilli strips and coriander, to garnish

1 Bring half the coconut milk to the boil. Add the yellow curry paste, stir until it disperses, then simmer for about 10 minutes.

2 Add the fish sauce, salt, sugar and remaining coconut milk. Simmer for a further 5 minutes.

COOK'S TIP

To make yellow curry paste, process together 6–8 yellow chillies, 1 chopped lemon grass stalk, 4 shallots, 4 garlic cloves, 15ml/1 tbsp chopped fresh root ginger, 5ml/1 tsp coriander seeds, 5ml/1 tsp mustard powder, 5ml/1 tsp salt, 2.5ml/½ tsp ground cinnamon, 15ml/1 tbsp light brown sugar and 30ml/2 tbsp oil.

3 Add the prawns and cherry tomatoes. Simmer very gently for about 5 minutes, until the prawns are pink and tender.

4 Serve immediately, sprinkled with lime juice and garnished with chillies and coriander.

Creole Fish Stew

A simple, attractive dish – good for an informal dinner party.

INGREDIENTS

Serves 4–6

2 whole red bream or large snapper,
  cleaned and cut into 2.5cm/1in pieces
30ml/2 tbsp spice seasoning
30ml/2 tbsp malt vinegar
flour, for dusting
oil, for frying

For the sauce
30ml/2 tbsp vegetable oil
15g/½oz butter or margarine
1 onion, finely chopped
275g/10oz fresh tomatoes, skinned and
  finely chopped
2 garlic cloves, crushed
2 thyme sprigs
600ml/1 pint/2½ cups fish stock or water
2.5ml/½ tsp ground cinnamon
1 hot chilli, chopped
115g/4oz red pepper, finely chopped
115g/4oz green pepper, finely chopped
salt
oregano sprigs, to garnish

1 Sprinkle the fish with the spice seasoning and vinegar, turning to coat. Set aside in the refrigerator to marinate for a minimum of 2 hours or overnight.

2 When ready to cook, place a little flour on a large plate and coat the fish pieces, shaking off any excess flour.

3 Heat a little oil in a large frying pan and fry the fish pieces for about 5 minutes, until golden brown, then set aside. Do not worry if the fish is not cooked through, it will finish cooking in the sauce.

4 To make the sauce, heat the oil and butter or margarine in a large frying pan or wok and stir-fry the onion for 5 minutes. Add the tomatoes, garlic and thyme, stir well and simmer for a further 5 minutes. Stir in the stock or water, cinnamon and hot chilli.

5 Add the fish pieces and the chopped red and green peppers. Simmer until the fish is cooked through and the stock has reduced to a thick sauce. Adjust the seasoning with salt. Serve hot, garnished with oregano.

Indian Fish Stew

A spicy fish stew made with potatoes, peppers and traditional Indian spices.

Serves 4

30ml/2 tbsp oil

5ml/1 tsp cumin seeds

1 onion, chopped

1 red pepper, thinly sliced

1 garlic clove, crushed

2 red chillies, finely chopped

2 bay leaves

2.5ml/½ tsp salt

5ml/1 tsp ground cumin

5ml/1 tsp ground coriander

5ml/1 tsp chilli powder

400g/14oz can chopped tomatoes

2 large potatoes, cut into 2.5cm/
   1in chunks

300ml/½ pint/1¼ cups fish stock

4 cod fillets

chappatis, to serve

1 Heat the oil in a large deep-sided frying pan and fry the cumin seeds for 2 minutes until they begin to splutter. Add the onion, pepper, garlic, chillies and bay leaves and fry for 5–7 minutes until the onions have browned.

2 Add the salt, ground cumin, ground coriander and chilli powder and cook for 3–4 minutes.

3 Stir in the chopped tomatoes, potatoes and fish stock. Bring to the boil and simmer for a further 10 minutes.

4 Add the fish, then cover and simmer for 10 minutes, or until the fish is tender. Serve with freshly cooked chappatis.

Tanzanian Fish Curry

A deliciously fragrant sauce full of tender fish.

Serves 2–3

1 large snapper or red bream
1 lemon
45ml/3 tbsp vegetable oil
1 onion, finely chopped
2 garlic cloves, crushed
45ml/3 tbsp curry powder
400g/14oz can chopped tomatoes
20ml/4 tsp smooth unsalted peanut butter
½ green pepper, chopped
2 slices fresh root ginger
1 fresh green chilli, seeded and
    finely chopped
about 600ml/1 pint/2½ cups fish stock
15ml/1 tbsp finely chopped fresh
    coriander
salt and freshly ground black pepper

1 Season the fish, inside and out with salt and pepper and place in a shallow bowl. Halve the lemon and squeeze the juice all over the fish. Cover loosely with clear film and set aside to marinate for at least 2 hours.

2 Heat the oil in a large saucepan and fry the onion and garlic for 5–6 minutes, until soft. Reduce the heat, add the curry powder and cook, stirring constantly, for a further 5 minutes.

3 Stir in the tomatoes and then the peanut butter, mixing well. Then add the green pepper, ginger, chilli and stock. Stir well and simmer gently for 10 minutes.

4 Cut the fish into pieces and gently lower into the sauce. Simmer for a further 20 minutes, or until the fish is cooked. Using a slotted spoon, transfer the fish pieces to a plate.

5 Stir the coriander into the sauce and adjust the seasoning. If the sauce is very thick, add a little extra stock or water. Return the fish to the sauce, cook gently to heat through and then serve immediately.

COOK'S TIP

The fish can be fried before it is added to the sauce, if preferred. Dip it in seasoned flour and fry in oil in a large frying pan or a wok for a few minutes before adding to the sauce.

Crab and Corn Gumbo

Gumbos are traditional Creole dishes, which come from New Orleans, Louisiana, and always contain a roux that gives this dish a distinctly rich flavour.

INGREDIENTS

Serves 4

25g/1oz butter or margarine
25g/1oz plain flour
15ml/1 tbsp vegetable oil
1 onion, finely chopped
115g/4oz okra, trimmed and chopped
2 garlic cloves, crushed
15ml/1 tbsp finely chopped celery
600ml/1 pint/2½ cups fish stock
150ml/¼ pint/⅔ cup sherry
15ml/1 tbsp tomato ketchup
2.5ml/½ tsp dried oregano
1.5ml/¼ tsp mixed spice
10ml/2 tsp Worcestershire sauce
2 corn cobs, sliced
450g/1lb crab claws
cayenne pepper
fresh coriander, to garnish

1 Melt the butter or margarine in a large saucepan over a low heat, add the flour and stir together to make a roux. Cook for about 10 minutes, stirring constantly to prevent burning, while the roux turns golden brown and then darkens to a rich, nutty brown. If black specks appear, the roux must be discarded. Turn the roux on to a plate and set aside.

2 Heat the oil in the same saucepan over a moderate heat, add the onion, okra, garlic and celery and stir to mix together. Cook for a few minutes, then add the stock, sherry, ketchup, oregano, mixed spice, Worcestershire sauce and cayenne pepper to taste.

3 Bring to the boil, then simmer gently for about 10 minutes, until the vegetables are tender. Add the roux, stirring it well into the sauce, and cook for a few minutes, until thickened.

4 Add the corn cobs and crab claws and continue to simmer gently over a low heat for about 10 minutes, until the crab and corn are cooked.

5 Spoon on to warmed serving plates and garnish with sprigs of fresh coriander.

Fisherman's Stew

A chunky, hearty stew that is warming in winter. The stock used here is especially aromatic, but if you do not have time to prepare it, use a basic fish stock instead.

Serves 4

6 streaky bacon rashers, rinded and cut into strips
15g/½oz butter
1 large onion, chopped
1 garlic clove, finely chopped
30ml/2 tbsp chopped fresh parsley
5ml/1 tsp fresh thyme leaves or 5ml/ ½ tsp dried thyme
450g/1lb tomatoes, skinned, seeded and chopped
150ml/¼ pint/⅔ cup dry vermouth or white wine
275g/10oz potatoes, diced
675–900g/1½–2lb skinless white fish fillets, cut into large chunks
salt and freshly ground black pepper
fresh flat leaf parsley sprig, to garnish

For the stock

225g/8oz white fish trimmings, including heads and bones
25g/1oz butter
1 shallot, finely chopped
1 leek, white part only, finely chopped
25g/1oz mushrooms, finely chopped
50ml/2fl oz/¼ cup dry white wine
600ml/1 pint/2½ cups water
bouquet garni, consisting of 1 thyme sprig, 2 parsley sprigs and 1 bay leaf
small strip of dried orange peel

1 First make the stock. Put the fish trimmings in a large bowl, cover with cold water and set aside for 1–2 hours, then drain and chop into small pieces.

2 Melt the butter in a heavy-based saucepan, add the chopped shallot, leek and mushrooms and fry gently over a low heat for 2–3 minutes, or until softened but not browned. Stir in the fish trimmings.

3 Add the wine and bring to the boil over high heat. Boil until reduced by half, then add the water and bring back to the boil. Skim the surface, add the bouquet garni and orange peel, lower the heat and simmer for 25 minutes. Strain the stock and set aside. Discard the vegetables, bouquet garni and orange peel.

4 Fry the bacon in a large saucepan over medium heat until lightly browned but not crisp, then remove the bacon and drain on kitchen paper.

5 Add the butter to the pan and gently fry the onion, stirring occasionally, for 3–5 minutes, or until soft. Add the garlic, parsley and thyme and cook for 1 minute more, stirring constantly. Add the tomatoes, vermouth or white wine and the strained fish stock and bring to the boil.

6 Reduce the heat, cover and simmer the stew for about 15 minutes. Add the potatoes, cover again and simmer for a further 10–12 minutes or until they are almost tender.

7 Add the chunks of fish and the bacon. Simmer gently, uncovered, for 5 minutes, or until the fish is just cooked and the potatoes are tender. Adjust the seasoning, garnish with the parsley and serve.

COOK'S TIP

It is worth taking the trouble to make fish stock. Fish trimmings are usually very cheap and sometimes even free, but do make sure that they are fresh. It is best to avoid oily fish, such as mackerel or sardines, but virtually all types of white fish are suitable. Remove any roe and gills before cooking, as these will make the stock bitter. Fish heads, in particular, yield the greatest flavour and nutritional content and bones are also useful. Do not overlook the value of prawn shells and heads, which, used on their own, make an aromatic and flavoursome stock for poaching shellfish. They add a surprising amount of strength to a basic white fish stock, too. Try experimenting with different types of fish; there is surprising variation in the flavour and body produced. The preparation and cooking take little time and it is worth bearing in mind that fish stock does not benefit from prolonged cooking, which will result in a bitter taste.

Seafood Stew

'Soups' – really stews – of mixed fish and shellfish are specialities of all Mediterranean countries.

INGREDIENTS

Serves 6–8

45ml/3 tbsp olive oil

1 medium onion, sliced

1 carrot, sliced

½ stick celery, sliced

2 garlic cloves, chopped

400g/14oz can plum tomatoes, chopped, with their juice

1 litre/1¾ pints/4 cups water

225g/8oz raw prawns, shelled and deveined (reserve the shells)

450g/1lb white fish bones and heads, gills removed

1 bay leaf

1 sprig fresh thyme, or 1.5ml/¼ tsp dried thyme leaves

4 black peppercorns

675g/1½lb fresh mussels, in their shells, scrubbed and rinsed

450g/1lb fresh small clams, in their shells, scrubbed and rinsed

250ml/8fl oz/1 cup white wine

1kg/2¼lb mixed fish fillets, such as cod, monkfish, red mullet or hake, cut into chunks

45ml/3 tbsp finely chopped fresh parsley

salt and freshly ground black pepper

rounds of French bread, toasted, to serve

1 Heat the oil in a medium-sized saucepan. Add the onion and cook slowly until soft but not coloured. Stir in the carrot and celery and cook for a further 5 minutes. Add the garlic, the tomatoes and their juice and 250ml/8fl oz/1 cup water. Cook over medium heat for about 15 minutes, until the vegetables are soft. Purée in a food processor or pass through a food mill. Set aside.

2 Place the prawn shells in a large saucepan with the fish bones and heads. Add the herbs, peppercorns and remaining water. Bring to the boil, reduce the heat, and simmer for 25 minutes, skimming off any scum that rises to the surface. Strain and pour into a pan with the tomato sauce. Season to taste.

3 Place the mussels and clams in a saucepan with the wine. Cover and steam until all the shells have opened. (Discard any that do not open.)

4 Lift the clams and mussels out and set aside. Filter the cooking liquid through a layer of kitchen paper and add it to the stock and tomato sauce mixture. Check the seasoning.

5 Bring the sauce to the boil. Add the fish and boil for 5 minutes. Stir in the mussels and clams and cook for a further 2–3 minutes. Transfer the stew to a warmed casserole. Sprinkle with parsley, and serve with the toasted rounds of French bread.

Italian Fish Stew

Italians are renowned for enjoying good food, especially if it is shared with all the members of an extended family. This stew is a veritable feast of fish and seafood in a delicious tomato broth, suitable for a more modest family lunch.

Serves 4

30ml/2 tbsp olive oil

1 onion, thinly sliced

a few saffron threads

5ml/1 tsp dried thyme

large pinch of cayenne pepper

2 garlic cloves, finely chopped

2 x 400g/14oz cans peeled tomatoes, drained and chopped

175ml/6fl oz/¾ cup dry white wine

2 litres/3¼ pints/8 cups hot fish stock

350g/12oz white, skinless fish fillets, cut into pieces

450g/1lb monkfish, membrane removed, cut into pieces

450g/1lb mussels in the shell, scrubbed and 'beards' removed

225g/8oz small squid, cleaned and cut into rings

30ml/2 tbsp chopped fresh basil or parsley

salt and freshly ground black pepper

thickly sliced bread, to serve

1 Heat the oil in a large, heavy-based saucepan. Add the onion, saffron, thyme, cayenne pepper and salt, to taste. Stir well and cook over a low heat for about 8–10 minutes, until the onion is soft. Add the garlic and cook for a further 1 minute.

2 Stir in the tomatoes, wine and fish stock. Bring to the boil and boil for 1 minute, then reduce the heat and simmer gently for 15 minutes.

3 Add the white fish fillet and monkfish pieces to the pan and simmer gently over a low heat for a further 3 minutes.

4 Add the mussels and squid rings and simmer for about 2 minutes, until the mussels open. Discard any that remain closed. Stir in the basil or parsley and season to taste. Ladle into warmed soup bowls and serve with bread.

Ragoût of Shellfish with Sweet Scented Basil

Green curry paste is an integral part of Thai cooking and can be used to accompany other dishes made with fish or chicken. Curry pastes will keep for up to 3 weeks stored in an airtight container in the refrigerator.

INGREDIENTS

Serves 4–6

450g/1lb fresh mussels in their shells, scrubbed and with 'beards' removed
60ml/4 tbsp water
225g/8oz medium squid
400ml/14fl oz/1⅔ cups canned coconut milk
300ml/½ pint/1¼ cups chicken or vegetable stock
350g/12oz monkfish, hoki or red snapper, skinned
150g/5oz raw or cooked prawn tails, peeled and deveined
4 scallops, sliced (optional)
75g/3oz French beans, trimmed and cooked
50g/2oz canned bamboo shoots, drained
1 ripe tomato, skinned, seeded, and roughly chopped
4 sprigs large-leaf basil, torn, and strips of fresh red chilli, to garnish
rice, to serve (optional)

For the green curry paste
10ml/2 tsp coriander seeds
2.5ml/½ tsp caraway or cumin seeds
3–4 fresh green chillies, finely chopped
20ml/4 tsp caster sugar
10ml/2 tsp salt
7.5cm/3in piece lemon grass
2cm/¾in piece galingal or fresh root ginger, finely chopped
3 garlic cloves, crushed
4 shallots or 1 medium onion, finely chopped
2cm/¾in square piece shrimp paste
50g/2oz coriander leaves, finely chopped
45ml/3 tbsp fresh mint or basil, finely chopped
2.5ml/½ tsp ground nutmeg
30ml/2 tbsp vegetable oil

1 Place the mussels in a large saucepan, add the water, cover and cook for about 6–8 minutes, until the shells open. Take three-quarters of the mussels out of their shells and set aside. (Discard any which have not opened.) Strain the cooking liquid and set aside.

2 To prepare the squid, trim off the tentacles beneath the eye. Rinse under cold running water, discarding the gut. Remove the 'quill' from inside the body and rub off the paper-thin skin. Cut the body open and score, criss-cross, with a sharp knife. Cut into strips and set aside.

3 To make the green curry paste, dry fry the coriander and caraway or cumin seeds in a wok to release their flavour. Grind the chillies with the sugar and salt in a mortar with a pestle or in a food processor to make a smooth paste. Combine the seeds from the wok with the chillies, add the lemon grass, galingal or ginger, garlic and shallots or onion, then grind or process until smooth.

4 Add the shrimp paste, coriander, mint or basil, nutmeg and vegetable oil. Combine well.

5 Pour the coconut milk into a strainer. Pour the thin part of the milk, together with the chicken or vegetable stock and the reserved mussel cooking liquid, into a wok. Reserve the coconut milk solids. Add 60–75ml/4–5 tbsp of the green curry paste, according to taste. You can add more paste later, if you need to. Boil rapidly until the liquid has reduced completely.

6 Add the coconut milk solids, then add the squid and monkfish, hoki or red snapper. Simmer for 15–20 minutes. Then add the prawns, scallops and cooked mussels with the beans, bamboo shoots and tomato. Simmer for 2–3 minutes, transfer to a bowl and decorate with the basil and chillies. Serve with rice, if you like.

Haddock and Broccoli Stew

This is an easy, one-pot meal full of colour and texture.

Serves 4

4 spring onions, sliced

450g/1lb new potatoes, diced

300ml/½ pint/1¼ cups fish stock or water

300ml/½ pint/1¼ cups milk

1 bay leaf

225g/8oz broccoli florets, sliced

450g/1lb smoked haddock fillets, skinned

200g/7oz can sweetcorn, drained

freshly ground black pepper

chopped spring onions, to garnish

crusty bread, to serve

1 Place the spring onions and potatoes in a large saucepan and add the stock or water, milk and bay leaf. Bring the mixture to the boil, then cover the pan and simmer for 10 minutes.

2 Add the broccoli to the pan. Cut the fish into bite-sized chunks and add to the pan with the sweetcorn.

3 Season the stew well with black pepper, then cover the pan and simmer for a further 5 minutes, or until the fish is cooked through. Remove the bay leaf and transfer to a serving dish. Scatter over the spring onion and serve hot with crusty bread.

COOK'S TIP

When new potatoes are not available, old ones can be used, but choose a waxy variety which will not disintegrate.

Hoki Balls in Tomato Sauce

This quick meal is a good choice for young children, as you can guarantee no bones. Its low fat content also makes it an ideal dish for anyone on a low-fat or low-cholesterol diet. If you like, add a dash of chilli sauce.

INGREDIENTS

Serves 4

450g/1lb hoki or other white fish
    fillets, skinned
60ml/4 tbsp fresh wholemeal
    breadcrumbs
30ml/2 tbsp snipped chives or
    spring onion
400g/14oz can chopped tomatoes
50g/2oz button mushrooms, sliced
salt and freshly ground black pepper
fresh chives, to garnish

1 Cut the fish fillets into large chunks and place in a food processor. Add the wholemeal breadcrumbs, chives or spring onion. Season to taste with salt and pepper and process until the fish is finely chopped, but still has some texture left.

COOK'S TIP

Hoki is a good choice for this dish, but if it is not available, use cod, haddock or whiting instead.

2 Divide the fish mixture into about 16 even-sized pieces, then mould them into balls with your hands.

3 Place the tomatoes and mushrooms in a large saucepan and cook over a medium heat until boiling. Carefully add the fish balls, cover and simmer for about 10 minutes, until cooked. Serve hot, garnished with chives.

Fish Stew with Calvados, Parsley and Dill

This rustic stew harbours all sorts of interesting flavours and will please and intrigue. Many varieties of fish can be used, just choose the freshest and best.

INGREDIENTS

Serves 4

1kg/2¼lb assorted white fish

15ml/1 tbsp chopped fresh parsley, plus a
    few leaves to garnish

225g/8oz mushrooms

225g/8oz can tomatoes

1 large bunch fresh dill sprigs

10ml/2 tsp flour

15g/½oz butter

450ml/¾ pint/1⅞ cups cider

45ml/3 tbsp Calvados

salt and freshly ground black pepper

1 Chop the fish roughly and place it in a casserole or stewing pot with the parsley, mushrooms, tomatoes and salt and pepper to taste. Reserve 4 dill sprigs to garnish and chop the remainder. Add the chopped dill to the casserole.

2 Work the flour into the butter with a fork. Heat the cider and stir in the flour and butter mixture, a little at a time. Cook, stirring, until it has thickened slightly.

3 Add the cider mixture and the Calvados to the fish and mix gently. Cover and bake in a preheated oven at 180°C/350°F/Gas 4 for about 30 minutes, or until cooked through. Serve at once, garnished with reserved sprigs of dill and the parsley leaves.

Coconut Salmon

This is an ideal dish to serve at dinner parties.

INGREDIENTS

Serves 4

10ml/2 tsp ground cumin

10ml/2 tsp chilli powder

2.5ml/½ tsp ground turmeric

30ml/2 tbsp white wine vinegar

1.5ml/¼ tsp salt

4 salmon steaks, about 175g/6oz each

45ml/3 tbsp oil

1 onion, chopped

2 fresh green chillies, seeded and chopped

2 garlic cloves, crushed

2.5cm/1in piece fresh root ginger, grated

5ml/1 tsp ground coriander

175ml/6fl oz/¾ cup coconut milk

fresh coriander sprigs, to garnish

spring onion rice, to serve

1 Mix 5ml/1 tsp of the ground cumin together with the chilli powder, turmeric, vinegar and salt. Rub the paste over the salmon steaks and leave to marinate for about 15 minutes.

2 Heat the oil in a large deep-sided frying pan and fry the onion, chillies, garlic and ginger for 5–6 minutes. Put into a food processor or blender and process to a paste.

3 Return the paste to the pan. Add the remaining cumin, the coriander and coconut milk. Bring to the boil, lower the heat and simmer for 5 minutes.

4 Add the salmon. Cover and cook for 15 minutes, until the fish is tender. Transfer to a serving dish and garnish with coriander. Serve with spring onion rice.

COOK'S TIP

If coconut milk is unavailable, dissolve some grated creamed coconut in boiling water and strain into a jug.

Moroccan Fish Tagine

Tagine is actually the name of the large Moroccan cooking pot used for this type of cooking, but you can use an ordinary casserole instead.

INGREDIENTS

Serves 4

2 garlic cloves, crushed

30ml/2 tbsp ground cumin

30ml/2 tbsp paprika

1 small, fresh red chilli (optional)

30ml/2 tbsp tomato purée

60ml/4 tbsp lemon juice

4 whiting or cod cutlets, about 175g/
   6oz each

350g/12oz tomatoes, sliced

2 green peppers, seeded and thinly sliced

salt and freshly ground black pepper

chopped fresh coriander, to garnish

broccoli, to serve

1 Mix together the garlic, cumin, paprika, chilli, if using, tomato purée and lemon juice. Spread this mixture over the fish, then cover and chill for about 30 minutes to let the flavour penetrate.

COOK'S TIP

If you are preparing this dish for a dinner party, it can be assembled completely and stored in the refrigerator, ready to bake when needed.

2 Arrange half the tomatoes and half the green peppers in a baking dish. Season with salt and pepper to taste.

3 Cover with the fish, in a single layer, then arrange the remaining tomatoes and green peppers on top. Cover the baking dish with foil and bake in a preheated oven at 200°C/400°F/ Gas 6 for about 45 minutes. Garnish with chopped coriander and serve with broccoli.

Octopus and Red Wine Stew

Unless you are happy to clean and prepare octopus for this Greek dish, buy one that is ready for cooking.

Serves 4

900g/2lb prepared octopus
450g/1lb onions, sliced
2 bay leaves
450g/1lb ripe tomatoes
60ml/4 tbsp olive oil
4 garlic cloves, crushed
5ml/1 tsp caster sugar
15ml/1 tbsp chopped fresh oregano
    or rosemary
30ml/2 tbsp chopped fresh parsley
150ml/¼ pint/⅔ cup red wine
30ml/2 tbsp red wine vinegar
chopped fresh herbs, to garnish
warm bread and pine nuts, to serve

1 Put the octopus in a saucepan of gently simmering water with one-quarter of the sliced onions and the bay leaves. Cook gently for 1 hour.

2 While the octopus is cooking, plunge the tomatoes into boiling water for 30 seconds, then refresh in cold water. Peel away the skins and chop roughly.

3 Drain the octopus and, using a sharp knife, cut it into bite-sized pieces. Discard the onions and bay leaves.

4 Heat the oil in a saucepan and fry the octopus, the remaining chopped onions and the crushed garlic for 3 minutes. Add the tomatoes, sugar, oregano or rosemary, parsley, wine and vinegar and cook, stirring constantly, for 5 minutes until the mixture is pulpy.

5 Cover the pan and cook over the lowest possible heat for about 1½ hours, until the sauce is thickened and the octopus is tender. Garnish with fresh herbs and serve with plenty of warm bread and pine nuts to scatter over the top.

Index

NOTES

NOTES

NOTES

NOTES

NOTES

NOTES